MEDICAL
SPANISH

MEDICAL SPANISH

Third Edition

GAIL L. BONGIOVANNI, M.D.

McGRAW-HILL
Health Professions Division
New York   St. Louis   San Francisco   Auckland   Bogotá
Caracas   Lisbon   London   Madrid   Mexico   Milan
Montreal   New Delhi   Paris   San Juan   Singapore
Sydney   Tokyo   Toronto

McGraw-Hill

*A Division of The **McGraw·Hill** Companies*

MEDICAL SPANISH, 3/e
Copyright © 2000, 1991, 1978, by The McGraw-Hill Companies, Inc. All rights reserved. Printed in the United States of America. Except as permitted under the United States Copyright Act of 1976, no part of this publication may be reproduced or distributed in any form or by any means, or stored in a data base or retrieval system, without the prior written permission of the publisher.

2 3 4 5 6 7 8 9 0 DOC DOC 0 9 8 7 6 5 4 3 2 1

This book was set in Souvenir by Better Graphics. The editors were John Dolan and Peter McCurdy. The indexer was Janet Perlman. The cover was designed by P.J. Smith. The production supervisor was Richard Ruzycka.
R. R. Donnelley & Sons Company was printer and binder.

This book is printed on acid-free paper.

ISBN 0-07-134550-7

Cataloging-in-Publication Data is on file for this title at the Library of Congress.

To My Parents . . . because of the love and respect we share.

Contents

Preface

Medical Spanish was written to express my gratitude to those people of Spain and Latin America who, since 1967, have given me the opportunity to share their language and their spirit of life.

Since its first publication in 1978, *Medical Spanish* has assisted English-speaking medical personnel as they tried to communicate and administer health care to their Spanish-speaking patients.

This third edition of *Medical Spanish* continues the comprehensive yet simple linguistic approach that allows medical personnel to take a thorough medical history and perform a complete medical examination on their Spanish-speaking patients.

To keep current with the changing specialties in medicine, I have added a chapter on the new specialty of Geriatric Medicine. Included are focus areas specifically related to the growing geriatric population.

I am pleased to include another new chapter, The Psychiatric Interview, prepared by Dr. Raphael J. Leo, Medical Director, Consultation-Liaison Psychiatry, Assistant Professor, Department of Psychiatry, State University of New York at Buffalo. This is an in-depth psychiatric evaluation covering all major psychiatric problems. My special thanks to Dr. Leo for his contribution to *Medical Spanish*.

MEDICAL
SPANISH

Chapter 1
HOW TO USE
THIS BOOK

Medical Spanish, formerly entitled *Entre doctor y paciente*,[1] was written to aid English-speaking medical personnel working with Spanish-speaking patients. This book is intended to provide a practical method for improving communication.

This book was originally prepared in Guatemala City, Guatemala. Practical trials were carried out for two months at Roosevelt Hospital, Guatemala City, where effectiveness of the text was tested in patient interviews.

1.1 ENGLISH INTO SPANISH

The vocabulary presented is representative of Spanish as it is spoken in Spain and Latin America. The English phrases have not always been given a literal translation. Instead, the Spanish words

---

[1]*Between Doctor and Patient.*

and phrases have been chosen to communicate the sense of the English questions in a way that will be understood by the patient.

Example:

I am going to examine your . . .	Voy a examinarle su . . .

1 abdomen*.	1 *estómago* (stomach).

Here the English word "abdomen" is translated as "estómago" (stomach). Wherever such free translating is done, the words involved are marked by an asterisk, and the literal translation of the Spanish word is given in parentheses. In this way, the interviewer will not read one word in English and think the same word has been translated literally into Spanish.

In order to keep the English and the Spanish phrases structurally similar, it was necessary, in some instances, to use a slightly awkward English wording. The Spanish phrase, however, is worded correctly and naturally.

Example:

Is the diarrhea . . .	La *diarrea es* . . .
1 of what color?	1 de qué *color?*
2 with blood?	2 con *sangre?*
3 with fat?	3 con *grasa?*

Thus, if interviewers follow the Spanish translation presented in the text, they will be speaking grammatically and idiomatically.

1.2 ORGANIZATION OF THE BOOK

The text is divided into fourteen chapters. Several chapters have been subdivided into sections to facilitate the collection of information. For the chapters on review of systems and physical examination, each section is devoted to one organ system. Certain sections have been further subdivided.

Example:
Chapter 5 Chief Complaint or Review of Systems
Section 5.4 Gastrointestinal System
Section 5.4.1 Nutritional History

Chapter 2 introduces some essentials of Spanish grammar. The Appendix presents basic and supplemental vocabulary. The remainder of the text is to be used during an interview with a patient who comes to the clinic or hospital. The interview begins with questions about the patient's social and family history (Chapter 3). Questions on past medical history, review of systems, physical examination, general treatment and follow-up, and medical therapy are covered in Chapters 4 to 8. Three special chapters cover the topics of contraception, labor and delivery, and poisonings. Psychiatric evaluation and geriatric assessment are each separate chapters.

1.3   THE INTERVIEW FORMAT

For the interviewer with little knowledge of Spanish, a response to an open-ended question may be difficult to understand. To avoid confusion, the questions to the patient have been phrased so that they can be answered either "Yes" ("Sí") or "No" ("No"). Several variations on the yes/no question are also used. To round out the interview, a multipurpose request format, which is to be accompanied by appropriate gestures, is provided.

1.3.1   Basic Yes/No Question

Almost all questions in this book are phrased so that the patient may answer "Sí" or "No" as the interviewer reads them. Some questions begin with a repeating phrase to which a list of different words or phrases may be appended.

Example:

Do you often . . .   Tiene *frecuentemente*

1 feel nauseated?   1   *náusea?*
2 vomit?   2   *vómitos?*
3 burp?   3   *eructos?*

The interviewer is not supposed to *suggest* symptoms to the patient. He simply asks, "Do you often feel *nauseated?*" and *waits* for the patient to respond "Sí" or "No." Other questions give more detailed information, but the basic format is the same.

Example:

Do you have pain on urination . . .	Tiene *dolor* al orinar . . .
1 at the beginning?	1 al *empezar?*
2 the whole time?	2 *todo* el tiempo?
3 at the end?	3 al *terminar?*

This method may alter the usual dialogue between health worker and patient, but it also helps the interviewer obtain information. If the traditional "open-ended" question form is used, it is difficult to restrain the patient from speaking too rapidly, and the interviewer with a limited acquaintance with Spanish will be unable to understand the response.

Three variations of the yes/no question are also employed.

1.3.2 Double-Tense Question

This question format is very practical for someone just learning Spanish. By substituting verb tenses, the interviewer can use the "double-tense questions" to obtain twice as much information. With this method of questioning either the *chief complaint* or *review of systems* (Chapter 5) can be investigated. The interviewer uses the same questions, but changes the tense.

Example:

Do you have OR have you had . . .	Tiene O *ha tenido* . . .
1 pain in your chest?	1 dolor del pecho?
2 shortness of breath?	2 sensación de ahogo?
3 difficulty in breathing?	3 dificultad al respirar?
4 night sweats?	4 sudor por la noche?

This technique is easy to use and does not require the interviewer to learn a completely new vocabulary. In a very few instances, a question is illogical in one tense. The interviewer should be alert to this possibility and carefully select the tense to be used. The interviewer should *not* ask "Do you have or have you had. . . ." If the chief complaint is under investigation, the interviewer asks, "Do you have. . . ." If the review of systems is being covered, the interviewer chooses "Have you had. . . ."

1.3.3 One-Common-Phrase Question

Another variation of the basic yes/no question format is the one-common-phrase question. In this variation, the same introductory phrase is used with different words to elicit additional information.

Example:

Have you ever been hit in the . . .	Se ha *golpeado* en . . .
1 head?	1 la cabeza?
2 face?	2 la cara?
3 neck?	3 el cuello?
4 eyes?	4 los ojos?

This question format may change the usual dialogue between health worker and patient but, again, it does simplify and perhaps eliminate the difficulty an English-speaking person may experience in interpreting a Spanish answer.

1.3.4 Fill-In-the-Blank Question

This question format is a version of the one-common-phrase approach. On the basis of responses made previously by the patient, the interviewer can gain additional information simply by substituting the known information into the question.

Example:

In reviewing the cardiovascular system, the interviewer has learned that the patient has experienced "shortness of breath." To obtain additional information about this symptom, the blank in the question is filled in with the known symptom.

Was (Is) the *shortness of breath* accompanied by . . .	Además de la *sensación de ahogo*, tuvo (tiene) . .
1 fever?	1 *fiebre?*
2 trembling?	2 *temblores?*
3 sweating?	3 *sudores?*

In this example, the combined used of the double-tense question and the fill-in-the blank question provides the interviewer with more extensive information on the patient's problem.

1.3.5 The Multipurpose Request

The request format allows the examiner to communicate several different instructions with the same phrase. This type of presentation is particularly helpful during the physical examination. When using these questions, the interviewer must *actively point to or demonstrate* a particular item.

Example:

Please . . .	Por favor . . .
1 walk on THIS.	1 camine sobre ESTO.

This refers to a treadmill for the exercise tolerance test.

2 take THESE pills.	2 tome ESTAS píldoras.

These refers to a specific color or shape of the pills.

Whenever the multipurpose request is used in the book, the variable is shown in capitals as in the examples shown here.

The yes/no question, together with its variations, and the multipurpose request are employed to facilitate the interview, physical examination, and follow-up. This method of interviewing is simple and requires only that the interviewer be a more active participant in the clinic or a hospital visit. For those health workers with a greater knowledge of Spanish, the book provides an ample medical vocabulary, and it should not be difficult for such workers to incorporate the new vocabulary into their usual interview.

Effective communication in a linguistically simple style is the principal goal of this book. The interview format has been designed to minimize the interviewer's difficulty as he or she attempts to communicate in a new language with patients. The primary aim of *Medical Spanish* is to help the English-speaking health worker provide more reassuring and effective health care to Spanish-speaking patients.

Chapter 2
GRAMMAR AND PRONUNCIATION

This book is not intended to provide complete grammatical information. Therefore, there are only a few concepts to keep in mind about grammar and pronunciation.

The syllabic breakdown of the Spanish words is not given. It is recommended that the words be pronounced as they would be in English, keeping the few pronunciation rules in mind. The patient will understand even though the accent may not be perfect.

2.1 PRONUNCIATION

1 Spanish vowels:
   a is pronounced like "a" in *fAther.*
   e is pronounced like "ai" in *AIr.*
   i is pronounced like "ee" in *frEE.*
   o is pronounced like "o" in *lOw.*
   u is pronounced like "oe" in *shOE.*

2 When "a," "e," or "o" is followed by "u" or "i," the two vowels form a single sound with prolongation of the "a," "e," or "o" sound.

Example: causa (cause)[1]

When "i" or "u" precedes another vowel, the two vowels form one sound with slight emphasis of the second vowel.

Example: viuda (widow)

3 "B" and "v" are pronounced exactly alike in Spanish. They sound like the "b" in *aBolition*.

4 "Ch" is an independent letter of the alphabet and is pronounced like the hard "ch" in *CHeese*.

5 At the beginning of a word, "d" is like the hard "d" in *day*. In the middle of a word, "d" is pronounced like the "th" in *wiTH*.

Example: Todo (all) is pronounced "to-tho."

6 In Spanish the "h" is *always* silent.

Example: Hijo (son) is pronounced "ee-ho." All other letters are pronounced.

7 "J" is similar to the hard "h" in *horizon* and is slightly guttural.

Example: Joven (young) is pronounced "ho-ven."

8 A "ll" is pronounced like "ye" in *YEllow*.

Example: Llamar (call) is pronounced "ya-mar."

9 "Ñ" is a separate letter of the alphabet. It is pronounced like "ny" of *caNYon* and is nasal-sounding.

10 Single "r" at the beginning of a word and "rr" in the middle of a word are always trilled. This sound is made by vibrating the tongue against the roof of the mouth with a strong expulsion of breath.

11 If a word ends in a consonant other than "n" or "s," the stress is on the last syllable.

Example: ardor (burning)

Words ending in a vowel, "n," or "s" stress the second to the last syllable.

---

[1]The English translation is always enclosed in parentheses.

Example: ca<u>m</u>isa (shirt), <u>c</u>asas (houses)

Any word whose pronunciation differs from these rules will always have a *written accent*.

Example: médico (doctor), not medico.

2.2 GRAMMAR

1 Plurals of nouns are formed simply by adding "s" if the word ends in an unaccented vowel.

Example: dedo (finger)
          dedos (fingers)

or by adding "es" if it ends in a consonant, "y," or an accented vowel.

Example: dolor (pain)
          dolores (pains)
          ley (law)
          leyes (laws)
          rubí (ruby)
          rubíes (rubies)

2 The definite articles are:

Feminine   **Masculine**

Singular   Plural   Singular   Plural
la   las   el   los

Example: la pierna (the leg)
          las piernas (the legs)
          el brazo (the arm)
          los brazos (the arms)

3 In general, words ending in "o" are masculine and those ending in "a" are feminine. An adjective agrees in number and in gender with the noun it modifies.

Example: niña (girl)   las niñas enfermas (the sick girls)

niño (boy)   el niño enfermo (the sick boy)

One relevant exception to this rule is: la mano (the hand) rather than el mano.

4 *Possessive Adjectives:* Unless you are speaking to a child, you should use the formal address.

	Singular	*Plural*
(my)	mi	mis
(your familiar)	tu	tus
(his, her, your formal)	su	sus
(our)	nuestro (a)[2]	neustros (as)[3]
(your familiar)	vuestro (a)	vuestros (as)
(their)	su	sus

For parts of the body the possessive adjective can be replaced by the definite article. The meaning of the sentence remains clear.

Example: Levante su brazo. (Raise your arm.)

or

Levante el brazo. (still understood as, Raise your arm.)

5 *Subject Pronouns*

	Singular		*Plural*
(I)	yo	(we)	nosotros (as)
(you familiar)	tú	(you familiar)	vosotros (as)
(he)	él[4]	(they)	ellos (as)
(she)	ella		
(you formal)	usted[5]	(you formal)	ustedes

It is not always necessary to write the subject pronoun in a sentence. The conjugated verb is enough.

Example: Yo soy el médico. (I am the doctor.) can correctly be written, Soy el médico.

6 *Contractions*

al = a + el (to the)

del = de + el (of the) It also forms the possessive.

Example: Voy al hospital. (I am going to the hospital.)

la herida del paciente (the patient's wound)

(the wound *of the* patient)

---

[2]The feminine form is made by changing the final "o" to an "a."
[3]The plural is formed by adding "s."
[4]Notice the written accent on él (he) to distinguish it from el (the).
[5]Usted is abbreviated Vd., ustedes is abbreviated Vds.

7   *Common Suffixes and Prefixes*

a   *Diminutives:* "ito" (a) dolor (pain)
                        dolorcito (slight pain)

b   *Augmentatives:* "ísimo" (a) cansado (tired)
                           cansadísimo (very tired)

c   *Adverbs:* "mente" is added to the feminine form of the adjective to form the adverb.
    generosa (generous)
    generosamente (generously)

d   *"Dad" and "tad"* are equivalent to the English "ty."
    cantidad (quantity)
    facultad (faculty)

e   *"Ería"* denotes the location where something is made or sold.
    libro (book)
    librería (bookstore)

f   *"Ero"* (a) indicates the person who makes or sells the object.
    zapato (shoe)
    zapatero (shoemaker)

g   *"Des"* before a word forms the opposite of the original word.
    vestir (to dress)
    desvestir (to undress)
    agradable (agreeable)
    desagradable (disagreeable)

2.3   SPELLING

To spell any word in Spanish, write it exactly as it sounds, remembering that the "h" is silent. Normally, only three letters may be doubled in Spanish:

c   contracción (contraction)
l   ella (she)
r   hierro (iron)

Chapter 3
SOCIAL AND FAMILY HISTORY

3.1 GENERAL SOCIAL BACKGROUND

What is your name?
How old are you?
Where were you born?
When did you come to this country?
Where do you live?
How long have you lived there?
What is your address?
Have you lived in _____?
Do you live alone?

DATOS SOCIALES GENERALES

Cómo se llama usted?[1]
Cuántos años tiene?
Dónde nació?
Cuándo vino usted a este país?
Dónde vive?
Hace cuánto tiempo que vive allí?
Cuál es su dirección?
Vivió usted en _____?
Vive solo (a)?

---

[1]For the sake of simplicity, the inverted question mark, which should *precede* every question, has been omitted.

Do you live with your . . .

1 parents?
2 husband (wife)?
3 son (daughter)?
4 mother?
5 father?
6 uncle (aunt)?
7 grandfather
   (grandmother)?
8 cousin?
9 friend?
10 other relative?

Are you . . .

1 single?
2 married?
3 separated?
4 divorced?
5 widowed?
6 single, but living with
   your girlfriend
   (boyfriend)?

Do you consider yourself to
be

1 homosexual?
2 bisexual?
3 heterosexual?

Do you have any children?
How many?
What ages?
Have you ever been married
before?
How many different sexual
partners do you have in
a month?
Do you have anal
intercourse?

Vive con . . .

1 sus padres?
2 su esposo (a)?
3 su hijo (a)?
4 su madre?
5 su padre?
6 su tío (a)?
7 su abuelo (a)?

8 un (a) primo (a)?
9 un (a) amigo (a)?
10 otro pariente?

Es . . .

1 soltero (a)?
2 casado (a)?
3 separado (a)?
4 divorciado (a)?
5 viudo (a)?
6 soltero (a), pero vive con
   su novia (o)?

Se considera

1 homosexual?
2 bisexual?
3 heterosexual?

Tiene *hijos*?
Cuántos?
De qué *edades*?
Ha estado casado (a) *alguna
vez*?
Cuántos amantes tiene por
mes?

Practica coito anal?

Do you have . . .
1 primary education?
2 secondary education?
3 college education?
4 graduate education?
5 professional education?
6 vocational education?

Tiene . . .
1 educación *primaria*?
2 educación *secundaria*?
3 educación *universitaria*?
4 estudios *graduados*?
5 educación *profesional*?
6 educación *vocacional*?

Is your religion . . .
1 Catholic?
2 Protestant?
3 Jewish?
4 Baptist?
5 Mormon?
6 Evangelist?
7 Episcopalian?
8 Christian Science?
9 Jehovah's Witness?
10 Muslim?
11 Buddhist?
12 Hindu?

Su religión es . . .
1 Católica?
2 Protestante?
3 Judía?
4 Bautista?
5 Mormón?
6 Evangélica?
7 Episcopal?
8 Ciencia Cristiana?
9 Testigo de Jehová?
10 Musulmán?
11 Budista?
12 Hindú?

3.2 OCCUPATIONAL HISTORY

DATOS OCUPACIONALES

Are you employed?
Do you work outside your home?
What type of work do (did) you do?

Tiene empleo?
Trabaja afuera de su casa?

En *qué* trabaja (trabajaba)?

1 retired
2 teacher
3 secretary
4 housewife
5 salesperson
6 doctor
7 lawyer
8 engineer
9 student

1 jubilado (a)
2 maestro (a)
3 secretaria
4 ama de casa
5 vendedor (a)
6 médico, doctor (a)
7 abogado
8 ingeniero (a)
9 estudiante

10	architect	10	arquitecto (a)
11	accountant	11	contador (a)
12	farmer	12	campesino, agricultor
13	waiter (waitress)	13	camarero (a)
14	mechanic	14	mecánico (a)
15	factory worker	15	trabajador (a) de fábrica
16	truck driver	16	conductor (a) de camión
17	bus driver	17	conductor (a) de bus
18	taxi driver	18	conductor (a) de taxi

Where do (did) you work?

How long have you worked there?
What was your first job?
What other jobs have you had?
How long did you work there?
Why did you change jobs?
Are you happy in your work?
Why?

Do (Did) you work with . . .

En *dónde* trabaja (trabajaba)?

Hace *cuánto* tiempo que trabaja allí?
Cuál fue su *primer* empleo?
Qué *otros* empleos ha tenido?
Cuánto tiempo trabajó en eso?
Por qué cambió de trabajo?
Está *contento* (a) en su trabajo?
Por qué?

En su trabajo, está (estaba) expuesto (a) a . . .

1	lead?	1	plomo?
2	insecticides?	2	insecticidas?
3	chemicals?	3	substancias *químicas*?
4	paints?	4	pinturas?
5	plastics?	5	plásticos?
6	other synthetic materials?	6	otras substancias *sintéticas*?
7	drugs?	7	drogas?
8	dusts?	8	polvos?
9	animals?	9	animales?
10	birds?	10	pájaros?
11	radiation?	11	irradiación?

When?
For how long?
Do (Did) you use any
precautionary measures?
What?

Cuándo?
Por cuánto tiempo?
Toma (tomaba)
precauciones?
Cuáles?

3.3 HOBBIES AND SOCIAL ORGANIZATIONS

Do you enjoy . . .

1 sports?
2 reading?
3 movies?
4 music?
5 theater?
6 painting?
7 photography?
8 gardening?
9 carpentry?

Do you play an instrument?

Do you belong to groups of . . .

1 the church?
2 the school?
3 sports?

PASATIEMPOS Y ORGANIZACIONES SOCIALES

Le gusta . . .

1 el deporte?
2 leer?
3 el cine?
4 la música?
5 el teatro?
6 la pintura?
7 la fotografía?
8 la jardinería?
9 la carpintería?

Toca un instrumento?

Pertenece a grupos de . . .

1 la iglesia?
2 la escuela?
3 deportes?

3.4 INSURANCE AND ECONOMIC INFORMATION

Are you the sole financial support of your family?
About how much money do you earn a month?
Does anyone else in the family work?

SEGUROS E INFORMACIÓN ECONÓMICA

Es el *único* que sostiene a su familia?
Más o menos, *cuánto* gana mensualmente?
Hay alquién *más* en la familia que trabaja?

Who?
How much do they earn?
Do you receive financial
assistance from any . . .

1   other people?
2   organizations?

Do you have . . .

1   life insurance?
2   hospital insurance?
3   accident insurance?
4   Medicare?
5   other social assistance?
6   other public assistance?

Do you have an insurance card?

Please show it to me.
Do you have a primary care
doctor?
Who is it?

Quién?
Cuánto ganan ellos?
Recibe *ayuda financiera*
de . . .

1   alguna *otra* persona?
2   alguna *organización*?

Tiene *seguros* . . .

1   de vida?
2   para el hospital?
3   para accidentes?
4   de Medicare?
5   de otra asistencia social?
6   de otra asistencia pública?

Tiene una tarjeta de seguro
médico?
Por favor, muéstremela.
Tiene un médico general?

Quién es?

Chapter 4
PAST MEDICAL HISTORY

This chapter covers the traditional information needed for a complete medical background. There are questions on immunizations, foreign travel, and illnesses that may have been acquired abroad.

4.1 PAST HEALTH, HOSPITALIZATIONS, AND ILLNESSES

How has your health been up until now . . .

1 good?
2 fair?
3 poor?

ESTADO DE SALUD, HOSPITALIZACIONES Y ENFERMEDADES ANTERIORES

Hasta *ahora*, cómo ha estado su salud . . .

1 buena?
2 regular?
3 mala?

Do you have your own
doctor?

Tiene su *propio* médico?

What is his (her) . . .

Cuál es su . . .

1 name?
2 address?
3 telephone number?

1 nombre?
2 dirección?
3 *número de teléfono?*

When was the last time you
went to his (her) office?

Cuándo fue la *última* vez
que fue a la clínica
de su médico?

What was the visit for?

Por qué consultó a su
médico?

Have you ever been in the
hospital?

Ha estado en el *hospital?*

When was it?
Why were you there?
How long were you there?
Which hospital was it?
What is the address?
Have you ever had surgery?

Cuándo?
Por qué?
Cuánto tiempo estuvo allí?
En qué hospital?
Cuál es la *dirección?*
Ha sido *operado* (a) alguna
vez?

Did they operate . . .

Le *operaron* de . . .

1 on your tonsils?
2 on your appendix?
3 on your gallbladder?
4 on your large intestine?
5 on your small intestine?
6 on your uterus?
7 on your ovaries . . .
   a the right one?
   b the left one?
   c both?
8 on your prostate?
9 for a hernia . . .
   a inguinal?
   b umbilical?

1 las amígdalas?
2 la apéndice?
3 la vesícula biliar?
4 el intestino grueso?
5 el intestino delgado?
6 la matriz?
7 los ovarios . . .
   a el derecho?
   b el izquierdo?
   c ambos?
8 la próstata?
9 una hernia . . .
   a inguinal?
   b umbilical?

10 for cataracts?
11 on your kidneys . . .
   a for stones?
   b for removal?
   c for transplant?

Have you had . . .

1 chicken pox?
2 measles?
3 rubella?[1]
4 mumps?
5 whooping cough?
6 scarlet fever?
7 rheumatic fever?
8 tuberculosis?
9 hepatitis?

10 cataratas?
11 los riñones . . .
   a por piedras?
   b para remover?
   c por un transplante?

Ha tenido . . .

1 varicela?
2 sarampión?
3 rubeola?[1]
4 paperas?
5 tos ferina?
6 escarlatina?
7 fiebre reumática?
8 tuberculosis?
9 hepatitis?

4.2 IMMUNIZATIONS AND ILLNESSES ABROAD

INMUNIZACIONES Y ENFERMEDADES EN EL EXTRANJERO

Have you ever traveled outside this country?
When?
Where?
Were you sick?
Did you see a doctor?

What was . . .

1 the diagnosis?
2 the treatment?

Have you had vaccinations for . . .

1 diphtheria?
2 whopping cough?
3 polio?
4 tetanus?

Ha viajado *fuera* de este país?
Cuándo?
A dónde?
Se enfermó?
Le vió un médico?

Cuál fue . . .

1 el diagnóstico?
2 el tratamiento?

Le han puesto vacunas de . . .

1 difteria?
2 tos ferina?
3 polio?
4 tétano?

---

[1]The translation of rubella into Spanish is rubeola. This is not a copy error.

5	smallpox?	5	viruela?
6	typhoid fever?	6	fiebre tifoidea?
7	cholera?	7	cólera?
8	BCG?	8	BCG?
9	yellow fever?	9	fiebre amarilla?
10	rubella?	10	rubeola?
11	measles?	11	sarampión?
12	hepatitis A or B?	12	hepatitis A o B?

When were they?
When was your chest x-ray?

Where was it taken?

Were the results . . .

Cuándo?
Cuándo le tomaron su última *radiografía* del pecho?
Dónde se la sacaron?

Los *resultados* fueron . . .

1	normal?	1	normales?
2	abnormal?	2	anormales?

Have you been tested for tuberculosis?
When?
Who tested you?

Were the results . . .

Ha recibido la prueba de *tuberculina*?
Cuándo?
Quién le hizo la prueba?

Los resultados fueron . . .

1	positive?	1	positivos?
2	negative?	2	negativos?

Have you had a blood transfusion?

Ha recibido alguna transfusión de sangre?

4.3 SOCIAL HABITS

Do you ever have problems sleeping?
How is your appetite?

Do you smoke/Have you ever smoked . . .

HÁBITOS SOCIALES

Duerme *bien*?

¿Cómo está su *apetito*?

Fuma/Alguna vez fumó . . .

1	cigarettes?	1	cigarrillos?
2	pipe?	2	pipa?
3	cigars?	3	cigarros?

4 chewing tobacco?

5 marijuana?

How much do you smoke a day?

How long have you been smoking?

Have you ever tried to stop?

Would you like to stop?

Do you use/Have you used . . .

1 cocaine?

2 heroin?

3 other illicit drugs?

How long have you used it?

Have you ever tried to stop?

Would you like to stop?

Have you ever shared needles?

Have you ever shared needles with someone with . . .

1 hepatitis?

2 AIDS?

Do you drink . . .

1 beer?

2 wine?

3 whiskey?

4 coffee?

5 tea?

How much each day . . .

1 glass?

2 bottle?

3 cup?

4 rapé?

5 marihuana?

Cuánto fuma al día?

Hace *cuánto* tiempo que fuma?

Ha tratado de *dejar* de fumar?

Le gustaría *dejar* de hacerlo?

Usa/Ha usado . . .

1 cocaína?

2 heroína?

3 otras drogas ilicitas?

Hace cuánto tiempo que la usa?

Ha tratado de dejar de usarla?

Le gustaría dejar de usarla?

Comparte o ha compartido agujas?

Ha compartido agujas con alguien que sufre de . . .

1 hepatitis?

2 SIDA?

Bebe . . .

1 cerveza?

2 vino?

3 whiskey?

4 café?

5 té?

Cuánto bebe al día . . .

1 vaso?

2 botella?

3 taza?

Do you drink when you
are . . .

1 alone?
2 sad?
3 depressed?
4 happy?
5 in a social situation only?

Bebe cuando está . . .

1 solo (a)?
2 triste?
3 deprimido (a)?
4 alegre?
5 en una reunión social
   solamente?

Do you think you have a
drinking problem?
Would you like help?[2]
Do you use any drugs or
medicines?
Which ones?
Why do you use them?
How long have you used
them?
Who gave them to you?

Cree que tiene *problema* de
alcoholismo?
Quiere ayuda?[2]
Toma alguna *droga* o
medicina?
Cuáles?
Por qué las usa?
Hace *cuánto* tiempo que las
usa?
Quién se las dio?

4.4 PAST MEDICAL HISTORY OF THE FAMILY

ANTECEDENTES MÉDICOS FAMILIARES

Is your father (mother)
living?
What did he (she) die from?
How old was he (she) when
he (she) died?

Vive su padre (madre)?

De qué *murió?*
Cuántos años tenía al morir?

Have you or anyone in your
family had . . .[3]

Ha tenido usted o alguién en
su familia . . .[3]

1 high blood pressure?
2 hyperlipidemia . . .
   a high cholesterol?
   b high triglycerides?
3 heart disease?

1 *presión alta?*
2 hiperlipidemia . . .
   a *colesterol elevado?*
   b *triglicéridos elevados?*
3 enfermedad del *corazón?*

[2]See page 139 for further questions about alcohol use.
[3]If the answer is "si," then ask: Quién? (Who?)
                                    Cuándo? (When?)

4	myocardial infarct?		4	*infarto cardíaco?*
5	cerebral infarct?		5	*derrame cerebral?*
6	varicose veins?		6	várices?
7	thrombophlebitis?		7	tromboflebitis?
8	arteriosclerosis?		8	arteriosclerosis?
9	obesity?		9	obesidad?
10	kidney disease?		10	enfermedad de los riñones?
11	diabetes?		11	diabetes?
12	cancer? What type?		12	cáncer? Qué tipo?
13	bronchitis?		13	bronquitis?
14	tuberculosis?		14	tuberculosis?
15	asthma?		15	asma?
16	pneumonia?		16	neumonía?
17	bleeding tendencies?		17	tendencias a *sangrar?*
18	anemias . . .		18	anemias . . .
	a sickle cell?			a células *falciformes?*
	b thalassemia?			b talasemia?
	c iron deficiency?			c *deficiencia de hierro?*
19	convulsions?		19	convulsiones?
20	mental retardation?		20	retraso *mental?*
21	psychiatric problems?		21	problemas *psiquiátricos?*
22	emotional problems?		22	problemas emocionales?
23	glaucoma?		23	glaucoma?
24	congenital defects?		24	defectos congénitos?
25	venereal diseases . . .		25	enfermedades *venéreas . . .*
	a gonorrhea?			a gonorrea?
	b syphilis?			b sífilis?
	c herpes?			c herpes?
	d AIDS?			d SIDA?
26	allergies?		26	alergias?

Are you allergic to . . .

Tiene *alergia* a . . .

1	foods . . .		1	las comidas . . .
	a eggs?			a los huevos?
	b milk?			b la leche?
	c seafood?			c los mariscos?

2 medicines . . .
  a aspirin?
  b penicillin?
3 iodine?
4 contrast medium?
5 pollen?
6 dust?
7 animals . . .
  a dogs?
  b cats?
  c others?

What happens to you?
Do you get...
  a rash?
  b shortness of breath?
  c swelling?
Have there been any other
diseases?
Which ones?
Is there anything else you
would like to tell me?

2 las medicinas . . .
  a la aspirina?
  b la penicilina?
3 yodo?
4 medio de contraste?
5 el polen?
6 el polvo?
7 los animales . . .
  a los perros?
  b los gatos?
  c otros?

Qué le *pasa*?
Su fre de . . .
  a erupción?
  b falta de aire?
  c hinchazón?
Ha padecido de alguna *otra*
enfermedad?
Cuáles?
Hay algo *más* que quiera
decirme?

Chapter 5
CHIEF COMPLAINT OR REVIEW OF SYSTEMS

Chapter 5 begins with a section about pain. In those cases where a detailed analysis of pain and the accompanying circumstances is needed, this section should be consulted. All the organ system sections contain at least the basic questions related to pain. In this way, the interviewer does not always have to refer back to the first section to continue his (her) investigation.

The other questions found in Chapter 5 are necessary for a complete investigation of each organ system. The gastrointestinal system section includes a brief nutritional history. The reproductive system is divided into various subsections: venereal infections, breast examination and pap smear, menstrual history, sexual function, and menopause.

5.1 PAIN

Do you have OR have you had pain?
How long have (did) you had (have) it?

Did it develop . . .

1   slowly?
2   suddenly?

In this (Was that) the first time that you have (had) this type of pain?[1]
When was the first time?
How long does (did) the pain last each time?
Is (Was) it . . .

1   severe pain?
2   mild?
3   moderate?
4   sharp?
5   intermittent?
6   constant?
7   boring?
8   colicky?
9   shooting?

EL DOLOR

Tiene O ha tenido dolor?

Cuánto tiempo hace (hacía) que lo tiene (tenía)?

Se inició . . .

1   lentamente?
2   de repente?

Es (Fue) la primera vez que siente este dolor?[1]

Cuándo fue la primera vez?
Cuánto le dura (duraba) cuando le viene (venía)?
Es (Era) un dolor . . .

1   severo?
2   leve?
3   moderado?
4   agudo?
5   intermitente?
6   constante?
7   penetrante?
8   cólico?
9   fulgurante?

[1]Whenever using the past tense, ask "cuándo?" (when?). This is important throughout this chapter.

10	burning?		10	quemante?
11	cramping?		11	como un calambre?
12	pressurelike?		12	opresivo?

Where is (was) the pain?
Show me with one finger.
Has (Did) the pain changed (change) location?
Where did the pain begin?
Where does (did) it hurt . . .

Dónde le duele (dolía)?
Señáleme con un dedo.
Ha *cambiado* (cambió) de lugar?
Dónde le empezó?
Dónde le duele (dolía) . . .

1   the most?
2   the least?

1   más?
2   menos?

Does (Did) the pain radiate?
From where to where?

Se *corre* (corría) el dolor?
Hacia *dónde*?

Do (Did) you have the pain . . .

Tiene (Tenía) el dolor . . .

1   all the time?
2   in the morning?
3   in the afternoon?
4   at night?
5   before eating?
6   after eating?
7   while eating?
8   when it is (was) cold?

9   when it is (was) hot?

10   when it is (was) humid?

11   when you are (were) . . .
     a upset?
     b worried?
12   when you exercise (exercised)?
13   when you urinate (urinated) . . .
     a at the beginning?

1   *todo* el tiempo?
2   *por la mañana*?
3   *por la tarde*?
4   *por la noche*?
5   *antes* de comer?
6   *después* de comer?
7   *mientras* come (comía)?
8   cuando hace (hacía) *frío*?
9   cuando hace (hacía) *calor*?
10   cuando hay (había) *humedad*?
11   cuando está (estaba) . . .
     a molesto (a)?
     b preocupado (a)?
12   cuando hace (hacía) *ejercicio*?
13   cuando *orina* (orinaba) . . .
     a al empezar?

b the whole time?

c at the end?

14 when you defecate (defecated)?

15 when you have (had) sexual relations?

16 when you swallow (swallowed) . . .
  a liquids?
  b solids?
  c both?

17 when you . . .
  a stand (stood)?
  b sit (sat) down?

  c lie (lay) down?

  d walk (walked)?
  e climb (climbed) stairs?
  f bend (bent) over?

Is (Was) there anything that makes (made) the pain . . .

1 better?
2 worse?

What is (was) it?
Is (Was) there anything else that accompanies (accompanied) the pain?
Does (Did) the pain go away when you rest (rested)?
Do (Did) you awake at night from this pain?
Do (Did) you take anything for the pain?
Does (Did) it help?
Does (Did) it make it worse?

b durante *todo* el tiempo?

c al terminar?

14 cuando evacúa o *defeca* (defecaba)?

15 cuando tiene (tenía) *relaciones sexuales*?

16 cuando *traga* (tragaba) . . .
  a líquidos?
  b sólidos?
  c ambos?

17 cuando . . .
  a está (estaba) *de pie*?
  b está (estaba) sentado (a)?

  c *está (estaba)* acostado (a)?

  d camina (caminaba)?
  e *sube (subía)* escaleras?
  f se agacha (agachaba)?

Hay (Había) *algo* que . . .

1 lo alivie (aliviara)?
2 lo aumente (aumentara)?

Qué es (era)?
Hay (Había) otras *molestias* que acompañan (acompañaban) el dolor?
Se *alivia (aliviaba)* el dolor al descansar?
Lo *despierta* (despertaba)?

Toma (Tomaba) algo para el dolor?
Lo *alivia (aliviaba)*?
Lo *aumenta (aumentaba)*?

5.1.1   *Inflammation and Infection*

Inflamación e Infección

Do you have OR have you had . . .

Tiene O ha tenido . . .

1   swelling HERE?
2   redness HERE?
3   tenderness HERE?
4   a sensation of warmth HERE?
5   limitation of movement HERE?
6   stiffness HERE?
7   itching HERE?

1   hinchazón AQUÍ?
2   enrojecimiento AQUI?
3   dolor AQUÍ?
4   calor AQUÍ?

5   limitación de movimiento AQUÍ?
6   rigidez AQUÍ?
7   picazón AQUI?

Has pus drained from the wound?

Ha salido *pus* de la herida?

5.2   HEAD AND NECK

CABEZA Y CUELLO

Do you have OR have you had pain HERE?
What is (was) the pain like?
How long have (did) you had (have) it?
How long does (did) the pain last each time?
How often do (did) you have the pain?
Does (Did) the pain radiate?
From where to where?
Is (Was) there anything that makes (made) the pain . . .

Tiene O ha tenido dolor AQUI?
Cómo es (era) el dolor?
Cuánto tiempo hace (hacía) que lo tiene (tenía)?
Cuánto le dura (duraba) cuando le viene (venía)?
Con qué *frecuencia* lo tiene (tenía)?
Se *corre (corría)* el dolor?
Hacia dónde?
Hay (Había) *algo* que . . .

1   better?
2   worse?

1   lo alivie *(aliviara)*?
2   lo aumente *(aumentara)*?

What is (was) it?

Qué es (era)?

Have you ever been hit in the . . .

Se ha *golpeado* . . .

1 head?	1 la cabeza?
2 face?	2 la cara?
3 neck?	3 el cuello?
4 eyes?	4 los ojos?
5 ears?	5 los oídos?
6 nose?	6 la nariz?

Have you ever lost consciousness?

Ha *perdido* el conocimiento?

For how long?
When?
What happened?

Por *cuánto* tiempo?
Cuándo?
Qué le *pasó*?

Do you wear . . .

Usa . . .

1 glasses?	1 anteojos?
2 contact lenses . . .	2 lentes de *contacto* . . .
a for distance?	a para ver de *lejos*?
b for close-up?	b para ver de *cerca*?
c for reading?	c para *leer*?
d all the time?	d *todo* el tiempo?
e since when?	e desde cuándo?

Do you have OR have you had . . .

Tiene O ha tenido . . .

1 frequent . . .	1 frecuentemente . . .
a headaches?	a dolor de *cabeza*?
b earaches?	b dolor del *oído*?
c colds?	c catarros?
d stuffed-up nose?	d la nariz *tapada*?
2 many nosebleeds?	2 sangrado por la nariz?
3 many ear infections*?	3 salida de *pus* por los oídos (pus coming from your ears)?
4 burning of your eyes?	4 *ardor* en los ojos?
5 itching of your eyes?	5 *picazón* en los ojos?
6 tearing of your eyes?	6 *lagriméo* de los ojos?
7 redness of your eyes?	7 *enrojecimiento* de los ojos?

8 trouble breathing through your nose?
9 pain . . .
   a in your forehead?
   b under your eyes?
10 gums that bleed easily?
11 dentures?
12 frequent sores . . .
   a on your tongue?
   b in your mouth?

When was the last time you had a . . .

1 vision test?
2 hearing test?

8 *dificultad* al respirar por la nariz?
9 dolor . . .
   a en la *frente?*
   b *debajo* de los ojos?
10 encías que sangran *facilmente?*
11 dentadura *postiza?*
12 úlceras *frecuentes* . . .
   a en la *lengua?*
   b en la *boca?*

Cuándo fue el *último* examen especial de . . .

1 la vista?
2 los oídos?

5.3 CARDIOVASCU-LAR-RESPIRATORY SYSTEMS

Do you have OR have you had . . .

1 pain in your chest?

   Where is (was) the pain?
   What is (was) the pain like?
   How long have (did) you had (have) it?
   How long does (did) the pain last each time?
   How often do (did) you have the pain?
   Is it worse when you breathe?
   When you inhale/ exhale?
   Does (Did) the pain radiate?

SISTEMAS CARDIOVASCULAR-RESPIRATORIO

Tiene O ha tenido . . .

1 dolor de *pecho?*

   Dónde le duela (dolía)?
   Cómo es (era) el dolor?
   Cuánto tiempo hace que lo tiene (tuvo)?
   Cuánto le dura (duraba) cuando le viene (venía)?
   Con qué *frecuencia* lo tiene (tenía)?
   Es peor cuándo respira?
   Cuándo aspirate/ exhala?
   Se *corre (corría)* el dolor?

From where to where?
Is (Was) there anything
which makes (made) the
pain . . .
a better?
b worse?

What is (was) it?

2 shortness of breath . . .
  a while exercising?
  b at rest?
  c when you are (were)
    upset?
3 difficulty in breathing . . .
  a sitting?
  b standing?
  c lying down?
  d exercising?
  e at rest?
  f when you are (were)
    upset?
4 night sweats?
5 palpitations?
6 frequent colds . . .
  a in winter?
  b in spring?
  c in summer?
  d in fall?
7 a cough?
  Is (Was) it a dry cough?
  Is (Was) it productive?
  Is (Was) the phlegm . . .
  a foamy?
  b thick?
  c foul-smelling?
  d clear?
  e of what color?
  f abundant?
  g a little bit?

Hacia dónde?
Hay (Había) *algo* que . . .

a lo alivie (aliviara)?
b lo aumente
  (aumentara)?
Qué es (era)?

2 sensación de falta de aire?
  a al hacer *ejercicio?*
  b al descansar?
  c cuando está (estaba)
    molesto (a)?
3 *dificultad* para respirar . . .
  a sentado (a)?
  b de pie?
  c acostado (a)?
  d al hacer *ejercicio?*
  e al descansar?
  f cuando está (estaba)
    molesto (a)?
4 sudores por la noche?
5 palpitaciones?
6 catarros *frecuentes* . . .
  a en el invierno?
  b en la primavera?
  c en el verano?
  d en el otoño?
7 tos?
  Es (Era) *seca?*
  Es (Era) con *flema?*
  Es (Era) la *flema* . . .
  a espumosa?
  b espesa?
  c con *mal* olor?
  d clara?
  e *de qué* color?
  f abundante?
  g poca?

h blood-streaked?

h con *manchas* de sangre?

When do (did) you cough?
Do (Did) you have pain when you cough (coughed)?
Do (Did) you breathe easier after coughing?

A *qué horas* tose (tosía)?
Le *duele (dolía)* al toser?

Respira (Respiraba) *mejor* después de toser?

Is (Was) there any position that makes (made) it . . .

Hay (Había) *alguna* posición que . . .

1 better?
2 worse?

1 la *alivie (aliviara)?*
2 la *aumente (aumentara)?*

Is (Was) the _____ accompanied by . . .[2]

Se *acompaña (acompañaba)* _____ de . . .[2]

1 fever?
2 chills?
3 sweating?
4 tingling sensation . . .
   a in the face?
   b in the lips?
   c in the extremities?
5 dizziness?
6 nausea?
7 vomiting?
8 loss of consciousness?

9 fainting?
10 numbness . . .
   a in the lips?
   b in the extemities?
11 pain?

1 fiebre?
2 escalofríos?
3 sudores?
4 hormigueo . . .
   a en la *cara?*
   b en los *labios?*
   c en las extremidades?
5 mareo?
6 náusea?
7 vómitos?
8 *pérdida* del conocimiento?

9 desmayo?
10 adormecimiento . . .
   a de los *labios?*
   b de las *extremidades?*
11 dolor?

How many pillows do you sleep with?
Since when?
Have you ever noticed . . .

con *cuántas* almohadas duerme?
Desde cuándo?
Ha *notado* que . . .

---

[2]Whenever this question form is used, fill in the blank with any of the symptoms found previously.

1 swelling in your . . .
  a feet?
  b hands?
2 bluish color in your . . .

  a lips?
  b feet?
  c hands?
3 coldness in your . . .

  a feet?
  b hands?

What type of regular exercise do you do?

How many stairs (blocks) can you climb (walk) without getting . . .

1 short of breath?
2 pain in your . . .
  a legs?
  b chest?

Does the _____ go away when you stop?

1 se le hinchan . . .
  a los pies?
  b las manos?
2 se le ponen *morados* (as) . . .
  a los labios?
  b los pies?
  c las manos?
3 se le mantienen *fríos* (as) . . .
  a los pies?
  b las manos?

Qué tipo de *ejercicio* hace regularmente?

Cuántas escaleras (cuadras) puede subir (andar) sin tener . . .

1 una sensación de *ahogo*?
2 dolor . . .
  a de las piernas?
  b del corazón?

se *desaparece* _____ cuando para?

5.4 GASTRO-INTESTINAL SYSTEM

Do (Did) you have a good appetite?
How much do (did) you weigh?
What is the most/least you've weighed?

Do (Did) you eat . . .

1 more than usual?
2 less than usual?
3 the same as usual?

SISTEMA GASTROINTESTINAL

Tiene (Tenía) *buen* apetito?

Cuánto pesa (pesaba)?

Cuál fue su peso máximo/mínimo?

Come (Comía) . . .

1 *más* que los usual?
2 menos que lo usual?
3 *igual* que siempre?

Are (Were) you on a diet?
Do (Did) you want to gain weight?
Do (Did) you want to maintain your present weight?
Do (Did) you want to lose weight?

Has your weight . . .

1   increased?
2   decreased?

How much?
Do you have OR have you had pain in your abdomen?*
Where is (was) the pain?
Show me with one finger.
What is (was) the pain like?
How long have (did) you had (have) it?
How long does (did) the pain last each time?
How often do (did) you have the pain?
Does (Did) the pain radiate?
From where to where?

Is (Was) there anything that makes (made) the pain . . .

1   better?
2   worse?

What is (was) it?

Do you get . . .

1   indigestion from . . .
2   pain with . . .
    a alcohol?
    b spices?

    c coffee?

Está (Estaba) a *dieta*?
Quiere (Quería) *subir* de peso?
Quiere (Quería) *mantener* su peso actual?
Quiere (Quería) *bajar* de peso?

Su *peso* ha . . .

1   subido?
2   bajado?

Cuánto?
Tiene O ha tenido dolor en el *estómago* (stomach)?
Dónde le duele (dolía)?
Señáleme con un dedo.
Cómo es (era) el dolor?
Cuánto tiempo hace (hacía) que lo tiene (tenía)?
Cuánto le dura (duraba) cuando le viene (venía)?
Con qué *frecuencia* lo tiene (tenía)?
Se *corre* (corría) el dolor?
Hacia dónde?

Hay (Había) *algo* que . . .

1   lo alivie (*aliviara*)?
2   lo aumente (*aumentara*)?

Qué es (era)?

Le causa . . .

1   *indigestión* . . .
2   dolor . . .
    a el alcohol?
    b la comida *condimentada*?
    c el café?

d milk?   d la leche?
e fats?   e las grasas?

Do you have OR have you had problems . . .

Tiene O ha tenido problemas para . . .

1 swallowing?   1 tragar?
2 chewing?   2 masticar?

Do you often . . .   Tiene *frecuentemente* . . .

1 feel nauseated?   1 náusea?
2 vomit?   2 vómitos?
3 burp?   3 eructos?

When you vomit (vomited), is (was) it . . .

Cuando *vomita (vomitaba)* es (era) . . .

1 accompanied by nausea?   1 acompañado de *náusea?*
2 before eating?   2 *antes* de comer?
3 while eating?   3 *mientras* come?
4 immediately after eating?   4 *inmediatamente* después de comer?
5 several hours after eating?   5 varias horas *después* de comer?
6 not related to when you eat (ate)?   6 *sin relación* con la comida?
7 in large quantities?   7 mucho?
8 in small quantities?   8 poco?
9 similar in composition to what you have (had) just eaten?   9 *parecido* a lo que comió?
10 bloody?   10 con *sangre?*
11 green?   11 de color *verde?*
12 like coffee grounds*?   12 de color *café-negro* (color of black coffee)?
13 acidic in taste?   13 de sabor *ácido?*
14 bitter in taste?   14 de sabor *amargo?*

Have you ever noticed . . .   Ha notado . . .

1 black stools?   1 heces *negras?*
2 mucus in the stools?   2 heces *con moco?*

3 bloody stools?
4 fatty stools?
5 foul-smelling stools?
6 foamy stools?
7 clay-colored stools?

8 a yellow color to your skin or eyes?
9 itching of your skin?
10 a change in the color of your urine?
11 pain on defecation?
12 anal itching?
13 blood on the toilet paper?

Have you noticed any change in your bowel habits?
How often do you defecate?
When did you last defecate?

Do you have OR have you had . . .

1 constipation?
2 gas?
3 diarrhea?
4 urgency?
5 incontinence of stool?

Since when?
How many times a day do (did) you have diarrhea?
How many times a night?

Is (Was) it accompanied by . . .

1 pain?
2 intestinal cramps?
3 straining?
4 gas?

3 heces con *sangre*?
4 heces con *grasa*?
5 heces con *mal* olor?
6 heces *espumosas*?
7 heces de *color de arcilla*?
8 un color *amarillo* en la piel o en los ojos?
9 *picazón* en la piel?
10 un *cambio* del color de la orina?
11 *dolor* al defecar?
12 *picazón* del ano?
13 *sangre* en el papel higiénico?

Defeca *normalmente*?

Cada *cuánto* defeca?
Cuándo defecó por la última vez?

Tiene O ha tenido . . .

1 estreñimiento?
2 gases?
3 diarrea?
4 urgencia para defecer?
5 incontinencia del heces?

Desde *cuándo*?
Cuántas veces al día tiene (tenía) diarrea?
Cuántas veces en la noche?

Se acompaña (acompañaba) de . . .

1 dolor?
2 calambres *intestinales*?
3 pujo?
4 gases?

5 fever?	5 fiebre?
6 chills?	6 escalofríos?
7 nausea?	7 náusea?
8 vomiting?	8 vómitos?
9 relief after defecating?	9 *alivo* al *terminar* de defecar?

Is (Was) the diarrhea . . .

La diarrea es (era) . . .

1 of what color?	1 de qué *color*?
2 bloody?	2 con *sangre*?
3 with fat?	3 con *grasa*?
4 with mucus?	4 con *moco*?
5 very foul-smelling?	5 con muy *mal* olor?

When you finish (finished), do (did) you feel as if you still have (had) to defecate?

Al terminar, se queda (quedaba) con deseos de defecar?

5.4.1 *Nutritional History*

Historia Nutricional

Do you usually eat (drink) . . .

Generalmente come (bebe) . . .

1 bread?	1 pan?
2 rice?	2 arroz?
3 beans?	3 frijoles?
4 cereal?	4 cereal?
5 macaroni?	5 pastas?
6 green vegetables?	6 vegetales *verdes*?
7 yellow vegetables?	7 vegetales *amarillos*?
8 fruits?	8 frutas?
9 meats?	9 carnes?
10 fish?	10 pescado?
11 poultry?	11 aves?
12 sweets?	12 dulces?
13 cheeses?	13 quesos?
14 milk?	14 leche?
15 eggs?	15 huevos?
16 butter?	16 mantequilla?
17 margarine?	17 margarina?

Is there anything you don't eat because . . .

Hay *algo* que no come porque . . .

1 you don't like it?
2 it makes you feel bad?
3 you are allergic to it?
4 it's against your religion?

1 no le gusta?
2 le cae *mal?*
3 tiene *alergia?*
4 está *en contra* de su religión?

How many times a day do you eat?
When?
Who prepares the food?

Cuántas veces al día come?

Cuándo?
Quién prepara la comida?

Is the food usually . . .

Es la comida *normalmente* . . .

1 raw?
2 fried?
3 baked?
4 broiled?
5 boiled?
6 spicy?
7 greasy?
8 salty?

1 cruda?
2 frita?
3 horneada?
4 *asada* al fuego?
5 hervida?
6 picante?
7 grasosa?
8 *muy* salada?

How much liquid do you drink a day?
More or less.
Do you use any sugar substitute?
Do you take vitamins?
Why?
Which ones?

Qué cantidad de *líquidos* toma diariamente?
Más o menos.
Usa algún azúcar *artificial?*

Toma *vitaminas?*
Por qué?
Cuáles?

5.5 URINARY TRACT

SISTEMA URINARIO

Do you have OR have you had . . .

Tiene O ha tenido . . .

1 problems with your . . .
 a kidneys?
 b bladder?

1 molestias de . . .
 a los riñones?
 b la vejiga?

2 pain from your . . .
  a kidneys?
  b bladder?

Where is (was) the pain?
What is (was) the pain like?
How long have (did) you
had (have) it?
How long does (did) the
pain last each time?
How often do (did) you
have the pain?
Does (Did) the pain radiate?
From where to where?
Is (Was) there anything
which makes (made) the
pain . . .

1 better?
2 worse?

What is (was) it?

3 pain on urination . . .
  a at the start?
  b the whole time?

  c at the end?
4 burning on urination?
5 to urinate more
  frequently?
6 a feeling of urgency to
  urinate?
7 to urinate in larger
  quantities?
8 to urinate a lot at night?

9 difficulty starting the
  urinary stream?
10 an interrupted urinary
  stream?

2 dolor de . . .
  a los riñones?
  b la vejiga?

Dónde le duele (dolía)?
Cómo es (era) el dolor?
Cuánto tiempo hace (hacía)
que los tiene (tenía)?
Cuánto le dura (duraba)
cuando le viene (venía)?
Con qué *frecuencia* lo tiene
(tenía)?
Se *corre (corría)* el dolor?
Hacia dónde?
Hay (Había) *algo* que . . .

1 lo alivie *(aliviara)*?
2 lo aumente
  (aumentara)?
Qué es (era)?

3 dolor al *orinar* . . .
  a al empezar?
  b durante *todo* el
  tiempo que orina?
  c al terminar?
4 *ardor* al orinar?
5 orinar con más
  frecuencia?
6 *urgencia* para orinar?

7 orinar en *mayores*
  cantidades?
8 orinar *mucho* por la
  noche?
9 *dificultad* para empezar
  a orinar?
10 el chorro *interrumpido*?

11 a decrease in . . .
   a the size of the urinary stream?
   b the force of the urinary stream?
12 dribbling after urination?
13 Stress incontinence?

14 small stones in your urine?
15 cloudy urine?
16 pink urine?
17 urine like Coca-Cola . . .
   a at the start?
   b in the middle?
   c at the end?

Is (Was) the_____ accompanied by . . .[3]

1 fever?
2 chills?
3 malaise?
4 low back pain?

Have you ever involuntarily dripped urine when you . . .

1 laugh?
2 sneeze?
3 cough?
4 run?

5.6 REPRODUCTIVE SYSTEM

Do you have OR have you had pain HERE?

11 disminución . . .
   a del *grueso* del chorro urinario?
   b de la *fuerza* del chorro urinario?
12 *goteo* al terminar de orinar?
13 incontinencia de esfuerzo?

14 orina con *arenilla*?
15 orina *turbia*?
16 orina *rosada*?
17 orina color de *Coca-Cola* . . .
   a al empezar?
   b en el medio?
   c al terminar?

Se acompaña (acompañaba) _____ con . . .[3]

1 fiebre?
2 escalofríos?
3 *malestar* general?
4 dolor de la espalda?

Orina por gotas *involuntariamente* cuando . . .

1 se ríe?
2 estomuda?
3 tose?
4 corre?

SISTEMA REPRODUCTIVO

Tiene, O ha tenido dolar AQUI?

[3]Fill in the blank with any of the symptoms found previously.

What is (was) the pain like?
How long have (did) you had (have) it?
When was the last time?
How long does (did) the pain last each time?
Does (Did) the pain radiate? From where to where?

Is (Was) there anything which makes (made) the pain . . .

1 better?
2 worse?

What is (was) it?

Cómo es (era) *el dolor?*
Cuánto tiempo hace que lo tiene (tenía)?
Cuándo fue la última vez?
Cuánto dura (duraba) cuando le viene (venía)?
Se corre (corría) *el dolor?*
Hacia dónde?

Hay (Había) *algo que* . . .

1 lo alivie (aliviara)?
2 lo aumente (aumentara)?

Qué es (era)?

5.6.1 *Venereal Infections*

Do you have OR have you had a genital infection?

With the infection do (did) you have . . .

1 itching of your genitals?
2 burning of your genitals?
3 redness of your genitals?

4 inguinal swelling?
5 inguinal tenderness?
6 sores on your genitals?
7 pus from the sores?

8 vaginal secretions?
9 fever?

Have you *ever* had a test for . . .

1 syphilis
2 gonorrhea

Infecciones Venéreas

Tiene O ha tenido alguna *infección genital?*

Se *acompaña (acompañaba)* la infección con . . .

1 *picazón* de los genitales?
2 *ardor* de los genitales?
3 *enrojecimiento* de los genitales?

4 *hinchazón* de la ingle?
5 *dolor* de la ingle?
6 *úlceras* en los genitales?
7 *pus saliendo de las* úlceras?

8 *flujo* vaginal?
9 fiebre?

Le han hecho una prueba para . . .

1 sífilis
2 gonorrea

3 herpes	3 herpes
4 AIDS	4 SIDA

When?

Cuándo?

Were the results . . .

Los *resultados* fueron . . .

1 positive?
2 negative?

1 positivos?
2 negativos?

Where you treated?
With what?

Recibió *tratamiento*?
Con qué le trataron?

5.6.2 Breast Examination and Pap Smear

Examen del Seno y Papanicolaou

When was your last . . .

Cuándo fue su *último* . . .

1 breast examination?
2 Pap smear?
3 mammogram?

1 examen del seno?
2 Papanicolaou?
3 mamorgrama?

Were the results . . .

Los *resultados* fueron . . .

1 normal?
2 abnormal?

1 normales?
2 anormales?

Have you noticed . . .

Ha notado . . .

1 a change in the . . .
  a size of your breasts (nipples)?
  b shape of your breasts (nipples)?
  c consistency of your breasts (nipples)?
2 any secretion from the nipples?
3 any pain or swelling . . .
  a of your breasts?
  b of your nipples?
  c under your arms?

1 algún *cambio* en . . .
  a el *tamaño* de los senos (los pezones)?
  b la *forma* de los senos (los pezones)?
  c la *consistencia* de los senos (los pezones)?
2 alguna *secreción* de los pezones?
3 hinchazón *o* dolor? . . .
  a de los senos?
  b de los *pezones*?
  c *debajo* del brazo?

How many children do you have?

Cuántos hijos tiene?

Did you breast-feed them?
Are you breast-feeding now?

Les dio de *mamar*?
Está dando de mamar *ahora*?

Is your . . .

Está circunciso . . .

1 husband circumcised?
2 sexual partner circumcised?

1 su esposo?
2 la *persona* con quien tiene relaciones sexuales?

5.6.3 *Menstrual History*

Historia Menstrual

How old were you when your period began?
Do you still have it now?

A *qué edad* le vino su regla por primera vez?
Le tiene *todavía*?

When was your . . .

Cuándo fue su . . .

1 last period?
2 second to last period?

1 *última* regla?
2 *penúltima* regla?

Is your period usually . . .

Su regla *normalmente* es . . .

1 regular?
2 early?
3 late?

1 puntual?
2 adelantada?
3 atrasada?

How long does it last?

Cuánto tiempo le dura?

Do you have a . . .

Sale . . .

1 light flow?
2 heavy flow?

1 *poca* sangre?
2 mucha sangre?

How many? . . .

Cuántos (as) . . .

1 pads do you use a day?

1 toallas sanitarias usa cada día?

2 tampons?

2 tampones?

How many days pass between periods?
Do you bleed in between periods?

Cada *cuántos* días le viene?

Sangra *entre* sus reglas?

With your period do you . . .

Con su *regla* tiene . . .

1 gain weight?
2 have severe cramps?

1 *aumento* de peso?
2 cólicos *fuertes*?

3 have breast tenderness?

4 have swelling of your . . .
   a hands?
   b feet?
   c breasts?

5 have back pain?

6 become . . .
   a depressed?
   b emotional?

5.6.4 Sexual Function

Do you have OR have you had any change in your desire to . . .

1 make love with . . .

   a a woman?
   b a man?

2 masturbate?

Do you have OR have you had any problems with . . .

1 erection? . . .
   a There is (was) none?
   b Is (Was) it difficult to achieve?
   c Is (Was) it painful?

2 ejaculation? . . .
   a There is (was) none?
   b Is (Was) it difficult to achieve?
   c Is (Was) it premature?
   d Is (Was) it painful?
   e Is (Was) it bloody?

3 orgasm? . . .
   a There is (was) none?
   b Is (Was) it difficult to achieve?

3 *dolor* de los senos?

4 hinchazón de . . .
   a las manos?
   b los pies?
   c los pechos?

5 *dolor* de espalda?

6 tendencia a . . .
   a deprimirse?
   b estar *más* sensible?

Función Sexual

Tiene O ha tenido un cambio en su deseo de . . .

1 tener *relaciones sexuales* con . . .
   a una mujer?
   b un hombre?

2 masturbarse?

Tiene O ha tenido problemas con . . .

1 la erección? . . .
   a No *la* tiene (tenía)?
   b Le *cuesta* (*costaba*)?
   c Es (Era) *dolorosa*?

2 la eyaculación? . . .
   a *No* hay (había)?
   b Le cuesta (costaba)?
   c Es (Era) prematura?
   d Es (Era) dolorosa?
   e Es (Era) con sangre?

3 el orgasmo? . . .
   a *No* hay (había)?
   b Le cuesta (costaba)?

c Is (Was) it painful?
4 the quantity of genital secretions?. . .
  a Is (Was) it excessive?
  b Is (Was) it too little?

Do you have OR have you had pain during sexual relations . . .

1 before intercourse?
2 during intercourse?
3 after intercourse?

Are you content with your sexual relations?
Would you like to talk with a sexual counselor?

5.6.5 Menopause

Have you noticed . . .

1 any change in your periods?
2 hot flashes?

3 sweating?
4 dryness of your skin?
5 a decrease in vaginal secretions?
6 difficulty or pain with entrance of the penis?
7 tiredness?
8 that you are . . .
  a depressed?
  b nervous?
  c irritable?

You are going through menopause.
This is normal for a woman of your age.

c Es (Era) doloroso?
4 la *cantidad de secreciones genitales?* . . .
  a *Es (Era) excesiva?*
  b Es (Era) *poca?*

Tiene O ha tenido dolor durante sus relaciones sexuales . . .

1 *antes* del acto sexual?
2 *durante* el acto sexual?
3 *despúes* del acto sexual?

Está *satisfecho* (a) con sus relaciones sexuales?
Quiere hablar con un consejero sobre el sexo?

La Menopausia

Ha notado . . .

1 algún *cambio* en su regla?
2 sensación de *calor* en la cara?
3 que suda mucho?
4 *sequedad* de su piel?
5 *disminución* del las secreciones vaginales?
6 dificultad o dolor al entrar el pene?
7 cansancio?
8 que está . . .
  a deprimida?
  b nerviosa?
  c irritable?

Está pasando por la *menopausia.*
Es *normal* para una mujer de su edad.

The symptoms will pass by themselves.

Los síntomas pasarán por *sí solos*.

I can give you something to make you more comfortable.

Puedo darle *algo* para ayudarle.

5.7 ENDOCRINE SYSTEM

SISTEMA ENDÓCRINO

Do you have OR have you had pain HERE?

Tiene O ha tenido dolor AQUÍ?

What is (was) the pain like?

Cómo es (era) el dolor?

How long have (did) you had (have) it?

Cuánto tiempo hace que lo tiene (tenía)?

How long does (did) the pain last each time?

Cuánto dura (duraba) cuando le viene (venía)?

How often do (did) you have the pain?

Con qué *frecuencia* lo tiene (tenía)?

Does (Did) the pain radiate? From where to where?

Se corre (corría) el dolor? Hacia dónde?

Is (Was) there anything that makes (made) the pain . . .

Hay (Había) *algo* que . . .

1 better?
2 worse?

1 lo *alivie (aliviara)*?
2 lo *aumente (aumentara)*?

What is (was) it?

Qué es (era)?

Have you OR has anyone else noticed . . .

Ha notado O le han hecho notar . . .

1 a big change in your weight . . .
   a An increase?
   b A decrease?
2 any change in your skin? . . .
   a Is it darker?
   b Is it a finer texture?
   c Is it a rougher texture?
3 any change in your voice? . . .

1 un *cambio grande* en su peso? . . .
   a Ha *subido*?
   b Ha *bajado*?
2 algún *cambio* en su piel? . . .
   a Es *más* oscura?
   b Es *más* fina?
   c Es *más* áspera?
3 algún *cambio* en su voz? . . .

a Is it higher?
b Is it lower?

4 any problem . . .
a concentrating?
b sleeping?

5 any change in your breasts? . . .
a An increase in size?
b Secretions?

6 any change in the . . .
a quantity of your total body hair?
b quantity of hair on your head?
c color of your hair?
d texture of your hair?
e distribution of your hair?

7 any change in your periods?

8 any change in your facial features?

9 any change in your desire for sexual relations?

10 an intolerance to . . .
a the cold?
b heat?

11 that you are more tired?

12 that you are more nervous?

13 that you perspire more than usual . . .
a during the day?
b at night?

14 that you are more thirsty?

15 that you urinate more?

16 that you eat more?

a Es *más* alta?
b Es *más* baja?

4 algún *problema* en . . .
a concentrarse?
b dormir?

5 algún *cambio* en los pechos? . . .
a Han *crecido*?
b Han salido *secreciones*?

6 algún *cambio* en . . .
a la *cantidad* de pelo del cuerpo?
b la *cantidad* de pelo de la cabeza?
c el *color* del pelo?
d la *textura* del pelo?
e la *localización* del pelo?

7 algún cambio en su *regla*?

8 algún cambio en su *cara*?

9 algún cambio en sus *deseos sexuales*?

10 que no *aguanta* . . .
a el frío?
b el calor?

11 que se *cansa* más?

12 que se pone más *nervioso* (a)?

13 que suda *más*. . .

a por el *día*?
b por la *noche*?

14 que tiene *más* sed?

15 que orina *más*?

16 que come *más*?

17 that you eat more and
    do not gain weight?

When you were a child, did
you ever have radiation
to . . .
1 your head?
2 your neck?

Have you ever noticed a
lump in your neck?

5.8 HEMATOLOGIC SYSTEM

Do you have OR have you
had pain HERE?
What is (was) the pain like?
How long have (did) you
had (have) the pain?
How long does (did) the
pain last each time?
How often do (did) you
have the pain?
Does (Did) the pain radiate?
From where to where?
Is (Was) there anything that
makes (made) the pain . . .

1 better?
2 worse?

What is (was) it?
What is your blood type?
Do (Did) you bruise easily?

Do (Did) you bleed . . .

1 easily from . . .
   a your nose?
   b your gums?

17 que come *más* y no
    engorda?

De niño (a), recibió *radiación*
en . . .
1 la cabeza?
2 el cuello?

Ha notado una *masa* en el
cuello?

SISTEMA HEMATOLÓGICO

Tiene O ha tenido dolor
AQUÍ?
Cómo es (era) el dolor?
Cuánto tiempo hace que lo
tiene (tenía)?
Cuánto le dura (duraba)
cuando le viene (venía)?
Con qué *frecuencia* lo tiene
(tenía)?
Se *corre* (corría) el dolor?
Hacia dónde?
Hay (Había) *algo* que . . .

1 lo *alivie* (aliviara)?
2 lo *aumente (aumentara)*?

Qué es (era)?
Qué tipo de sangre tiene?
Se le hacen (hacían)
moretones sin causa
aparente?

Sangra (Sangraba) . . .

1 facilmente de . . .
   a la nariz?
   b las encías?

2 a lot from a cut?
3 for a long time?

2 *mucho* de una herida?
3 por *mucho* tiempo?

5.9 MUSCULO-SKELETAL SYSTEM

SISTEMA MÚSCULO-ESQUELÉTICO

Which hand do you use most . . .
1 the right?
2 the left?
3 both the same?

Qué mano utiliza *más* . . .

1 la derecha?
2 la izquierda?
3 *igual* las dos?

Do you have OR have you had . . .

Tiene O ha tenido . . .

1 any broken bones?
2 to wear a brace of any type?
3 muscle weakness?
4 trouble . . .

1 fracturas?
2 que llevar *corsé*?

3 *debilidad* muscular?
4 *dificultad* en las piernas para . . .
    a *subir* escaleras?
    b *levantarse* de una silla?

   a climbing stairs?
   b getting up from a chair?
5 muscle spasms?
6 pain in your . . .
   a bones?
   b muscles?
   c shoulders?
   d elbows?
   e wrists?
   f fingers?
   g hips?
   h knees?
   i ankles?

5 *calambres* musculares?
6 dolor en . . .
   a los huesos?
   b los músculos?
   c los hombros?
   d los codos?
   e las muñecas?
   f los dedos?
   g las caderas?
   h las rodillas?
   i los tobillos?

Where is (was) the pain?
What is (was) the pain like?
How long have (did) you had (have) it?
How long does (did) the pain last each time?

Dónde le duele (dolía)?
Cómo es (era) el dolor?
Cuánto tiempo hace que lo tiene (tenía)?
Cuánto le dura (duraba) cuando le viene (venía)?

Does (Did) the pain radiate?
From where to where?

Se *corre* (corría) el dolor?
Hacia dónde?

Is (Was) there anything that
makes (made) the pain . . .

Hay (Había) *algo* que . . .

1 better?
2 worse?

1 lo *alivie (aliviara)*?
2 lo *aumente (aumentara)*?

What is (was) it?

Qué es (era)?

5.10 NERVOUS SYSTEM

SISTEMA NERVIOSO

5.10.1 Cranial Nerves

Nervios Craneales

Do you have OR have you
had . . .

Tiene O ha tenido . . .

1 trouble smelling?

1 *dificultad* para sentir
los olores?

2 a sensation of . . .
a odd odors?
b unpleasant odors?

2 *sensación* de olores . . .
a raros?
b desagradables?

3 blindness?
4 blind spots?

3 ceguera?
4 *manchas negras* frente
a los ojos?

5 blurred vision?
6 double vision?
7 spots before your eyes?

5 vista *nublada*?
6 visión *doble*?
7 *manchas* enfrente de
los ojos?

8 pain behind your eyes?
9 trouble distinguishing
colors?
10 decreased sensation in
your face?
11 trouble chewing?

8 *dolor* en los ojos?
9 *dificultad* para
distinguir los colores?
10 *pérdida* de la
sensibilidad en la cara?
11 *dificultad* para
masticar?

12 trouble whistling?
13 trouble . . .
a opening your eyes?
b closing your eyes?

12 *dificultad* para silbar?
13 *dificultad* para . . .
a *abrir* los ojos?
b *cerrar* los ojos?

14	decreased taste sensation?	
15	taste sensations that are . . .	
	a odd?	
	b unpleasant?	
16	loss of hearing?	
17	difficulty in hearing?	
18	the sensation that noises are louder?	
19	ringing in your ears?	
20	trouble swallowing?	

Since when?[4]
Where?

Did it develop . . .

1 slowly?
2 suddenly?

Has it gotten . . .

1 better?
2 worse?

5.10.2 Sensory

Do you have OR have you had . . .

1 loss of tactile sensation?

2 trouble distinguishing . . .

   a heat on your skin?
   b cold on your skin?
3 tingling sensations?
4 numbness?

14	*dificultad* para sentir los sabores?	
15	*sensación* de sabores . . .	
	a raros?	
	b desagradables?	
16	*pérdida* del oído?	
17	*dificultad* para oír?	
18	la *sensación* de que los sonidos son más fuertes?	
19	*zumbido* en los oídos?	
20	*dificultad* para tragar?	

Desde *cuándo*?[4]
Dónde?

Se inició . . .

1 lentamente?
2 de repente?

La *molestia* ha . . .

1 mejorado?
2 empeorado?

Sensibilidad

Tiene O ha tenido . . .

1 *falta* de sensibilidad táctil?
2 *dificultad* para distinguir . . .

   a el *calor* en la piel?
   b el *frío* en la piel?
3 hormigueos?
4 adormecimiento?

---

[4]The following four questions are to investigate any symptoms found in motor and coordination, sensory and cranial nerves.

5.10.3 Motor and Coordination

Do you have OR have you had . . .

1 loss of coordination?
2 loss of balance?
3 dizziness? . . .
  a Did you spin around?
  b Did the objects spin around?

Movilidad y Coordinación

Tiene O ha tenido . . .

1 *pérdida* de coordinación?
2 *pérdida* del equilíbrio?
3 mareo? . . .
  a Daba usted *vueltas*?
  b Le daban *vueltas* los objetos?

5.10.4 Special

Do you have OR have you had . . .

1 loss of . . .

  a rectal control?
  b bladder control?
2 trouble speaking clearly?
3 trouble understanding what you are asked?
4 loss of memory for . . .

  a recent events?
  b past events?
5 trouble . . .
  a reading?
  b writing?
6 loss of consciousness?

Especial

Tiene O ha tenido . . .

1 *pérdida* del control para . . .
  a defecar?
  b orinar?
2 *dificultad* para hablar?
3 *dificultad* para entender lo que le preguntan?
4 problemas para *recordar* . . .
  a hechos *recientes*?
  b hechos *pasados*?
5 *problemas* para . . .
  a leer?
  b escribir?
6 *pérdida* del conocimiento?

5.10.5 Convulsions and Headaches

Have you ever been hit in the head?

Convulsiones y Dolores de Cabeza

Alguna vez le golpearon la cabeza?

Do you have OR have you had convulsions?

Tiene O ha tenido convulsiones?

When did you have your . . .

Cuándo tuvo . . .

1   first convulsion?
2   last convulsion?

1   la *primera* convulsion?
2   la *última* convulsión?

How often do (did) you have them?

Con qué *frecuencia* le vienen (venían)?

Are (Were) the convulsions preceded by . . .

Están (Estaban) *precedidas* por . . .

1   a special odor?
2   a vision?
3   a constant thought?
4   a strange feeling?
5   any pain?

1   un olor *especial?*
2   una visión?
3   un pensamiento *fijo?*
4   una sensación *rara?*
5   algún *dolor?*

With the convulsions do (did) you . . .

Con las *convulsiones* . . .

1   lose consciousness?

1   *pierde* (perdía) el conocimiento?

2   bite your tongue?

2   se *muerde* (mordía) la lengua?

How long does (did) each convulsion last?

Cuánto le dura (duraba) cada convulsíon?

After a convulsion, how long are (were) you . . .

Después de una convulsión, *cuánto* tiempo . . .

1   unconscious?

1   está (estaba) *inconciente?*

2   disoriented?

2   está (estaba) *desorientado* (a)?

Do (Did) you take medicine for the convulsions?

Recibe (Recibía) *tratamiento?*

What kind?
For how long?

Qué tipo?
Por *cuánto* tiempo?

Are the convulsions . . .

1 better now?
2 worse now?

Do you have OR have you had headaches?

Are (Were) they . . .

1 mild?
2 moderate?
3 severe?

Where is (was) the pain?
Does (Did) it radiate?
From where to where?
What is (was) the pain like?
How long does (did) the pain last each time?
How often do (did) you have the pain?
In what year did you first have the pain?
When was the last time?

Is (Was) there anything that makes (made) the pain . . .

1 better?
2 worse?

What is (was) it?

Is (Was) the pain preceded by . . .

1 a special odor?
2 a vision?
3 a constant thought?
4 a strange feeling?
5 nausea?
6 vomiting?

Ahora, las convulsiones han . . .

1 mejorado?
2 empeorado?

Tiene O ha tenido *dolor* de cabeza?

Son (Eran) . . .

1 leves?
2 moderados?
3 fuertes?

Dónde le duele (dolía)?
Se *corre* (corría) el dolor?
Hacia dónde?
Cómo es (era) el dolor?
Cuánto le dura (duraba) cuando le viene (venía)?
Con qué *frecuencia* lo tiene (tenía)?
En que año tuvo el dolor por primera vez?
Cuándo fue la última vez?

Hay (Había) *algo* que . . .

2 lo alivie (*aliviara*)?
2 lo aumente (*aumentara*)?

Qué es (era)?

Está (Estaba) el dolor *precedido* por . . .

1 un olor *especial*?
2 una visión?
3 un pensamiento *fijo*?
4 una sensación *rara*?
5 náusea?
6 vómitos?

Is (Was) the pain accom-
panied by other problems?
What?
Are the headaches . . .

1 better now?
2 worse now?

Siente (Sentía) otras
molestias con el dolor?
Cuáles?
Ahora, los dolores han . . .

1 mejorado?
2 empeorado?

Chapter 6
INSTRUCTIONS FOR THE PHYSICAL EXAMINATION

This chapter begins with the general instructions needed for the physical examination. These particular phrases are repeated only in those organ system sections where they form a large part of the patient's instructions.

As in chapter 5, each organ system has its own section. With the exception of the nervous system, each section contains complete instructions for the physical examination of that particular system. For the examination of cranial nerves II, III, IV, VI, VIII, and IX, the examiner should refer to section 6.2, *Head and Neck*. The other phrases in this chapter are self-explanatory. However, there are a few points to keep in mind. When the instructions are linguistically complicated, as in the examination of the ocular fundus, the instructions are divided into single phrases. The examiner must remember to employ all the expressions needed to communicate the entire instruction.

Example:	
Please . . .	Por favor . . .
1 focus HERE.	1 mire AQUÍ.
2 don't move your eyes.	2 *no* mueva los ojos.
3 don't move your head.	3 no mueva la cabeza.
4 don't blink.	4 *no* parpadee.
5 look into the light.	5 *mire* la luz.

The sections for the urinary tract and the endocrine system are short because of the use of laboratory examinations for diagnosis. There are no instructions for the physical examination of the hematologic system, since this examination is almost exclusively based on observation and laboratory tests.

6.1 GENERAL INSTRUCTIONS	**INSTRUCCIONES GENERALES**
I am going to examine you.	Voy a *examinarle*.
Please undress except for your underwear.	Por favor desvístase *menos* su ropa interior.
Please undress completely.	Por favor, desvístase completamente.
Please put this gown on with the opening in the . . .	Por favor, póngase la bota con la abertura . . .
1 front.	1 en frente.
2 back.	2 atrás.
Please . . .	Por favor . . .
1 lie down.	1 acuéstese.

2	sit down.	2	siéntese.
3	stand up.	3	levántese.
4	bend over forward.	4	dóblese hacia *adelante*.
5	bend over backward.	5	dóblese hacia *atrás*.
6	lean forward.	6	inclínese hacia *adelante*.
7	lean backward.	7	inclínese hacia *atrás*.
8	lie on your . . .	8	acuéstese . . .
	a right side.		a sobre el lado *derecho*.
	b left side.		b sobre el lado *izquierdo*.
	c. stomach.		c boca *abajo*.
	d back.		d boca *arriba*.
9	turn your head . . .	9	*mueva* la cabeza . . .
	a to the right.		a a la *derecha*.
	b to the left.		b a la *izquierda*.
10	bend your head.	10	*doble* la cabeza.
11	turn over.	11	dése *vuelta*.
12	don't talk.	12	no hable.
13	lie still.	13	quédese *quieto* (a).

Please do THIS. — Por favor, haga ESTO.
Relax. — Cálmese.
Are you comfortable? — Está *cómodo* (a)?
THIS won't hurt. — ESTO no le dolerá.
Does THIS hurt? — Le duele ESTO?
Can you feel IT? — Puede sentirLO?
I'm sorry if THIS makes you uncomfortable. — Lo siento si ESTO le molesta.
It will only take a moment longer. — Solo un momento *más*.
That's enough. — Suficiente.
Once more. — *Otra vez*.
Very good. — Muy *bien*.
Thank you. — *Gracias*.
You may get dressed now. — Puede *vestirse*.
I will talk with you when you are finished. — Hablaré con usted cuando *termine*.

6.2 HEAD AND NECK

EXAMEN FÍSICO DE LA CABEZA Y EL CUELLO

I am going to examine your . . .

Voy a *examinarle* . . .

1 head.
2 eyes.
3 ears.
4 nose.
5 mouth.
6 throat.
7 neck.

1 la cabeza.
2 los ojos.
3 los oídos.
4 la nariz.
5 la boca.
6 la garganta.
7 el cuello.

Do you have pain when I bend your neck?
Please swallow.
Again.

Tiene *dolor* cuando le doblo el cuello?
Por favor *trague*.
Otra vez.

Please . . .

Por favor . . .

1 read THIS.
2 how many fingers do you see?
3 follow my finger with your eyes.
4 don't move your head.
5 cover your eye like THIS.
6 where do you see my finger?
7 focus HERE.
8 don't move your eyes.
9 don't blink.
10 look into the light.
11 open your eyes.
12 close your eyes.
13 look . . .
 a up.
 b down.

1 lea ESTO.
2 *cuántos* dedos ve?
3 *siga* mi dedo con los ojos.
4 no *mueva* la cabeza.
5 tápese el ojo ASÍ.
6 *dónde* ve mi dedo?
7 mire AQUÍ.
8 *no* mueva los ojos.
9 *no* parpadee.
10 *mire* la luz.
11 *abra* los ojos.
12 *cierre* los ojos.
13 *mire* . . .
 a arriba.
 b abajo.

c to the side.
d HERE.

I will touch your eye with THIS.
Don't be afraid.

Please tell me . . .

1 when you . . .
  a can hear THIS.
  b cannot hear THIS.
  c can feel THIS.
  d cannot feel THIS.
2 if THIS is . . .
  a louder in one ear.
  b softer in one ear.
  c equal in both ears.

Breathe through your nose.

Please . . .

1 open your mouth wider.
2 stick out your tongue.
3 say "ah."
4 move your tongue from side to side.
5 lift up your tongue.

c al lado.
d AQUÍ.

Voy a tocar el ojo con ESTO.
No tenga miedo.

Por favor dígame . . .

1 cuando . . .
  a pueda oir ESTO.
  b no pueda oir ESTO.
  c pueda sentir ESTO.
  d no pueda sentir ESTO.
2 si ESTO es . . .
  a más fuerte en un oído.
  b más suave en un oído.
  c igual en ambos oídos.

Respire por la nariz.

Por favor . . .

1 abra la boca más.
2 saque la lengua.
3 diga "ah."
4 mueva la lengua de lada a lado.
5 levante la lengua.

6.3 CARDIOVASCULAR-RESPIRATORY SYSTEMS

EXAMEN FÍSICO DE LOS SISTEMAS CARDIOVASCULAR-RESPIRATORIO

I am going to . . .

1 examine your lungs.

2 examine your heart.
3 take your pulse.
4 take your blood pressure.

Voy a . . .

1 examinarle los pulmones.
2 examinarle el corazón.
3 tomarle el pulso.
4 tomarle la presión.

Please . . .

1 sit down.
2 lean forward.

3 lie down.
4 lie on your . . .
   a right side.
   b left side.
5 stand up.
6 don't talk.
7 breathe deeply through your mouth, . . . again.

8 inspire.
9 hold it.
10 exhale.
11 take a deep breath.
12 relax.
13 breathe normally.
14 cough.
15 say "33."
16 say "e."
17 climb THESE stairs.
18 walk on THIS.

Do you feel dizzy?

Por favor . . .

1 siéntese.
2 inclínese hacia *adelante*.
3 acuéstese.
4 *acuéstese* sobre . . .
   a su lado *derecho*.
   b su lado *izquierdo*.
5 levántese.
6 *no* hable.
7 respire *profundo* con la boca abierta, . . . otra vez.

8 inspire.
9 *no* saque el aire.
10 exhale.
11 respire *profundo*.
12 descanse.
13 respire *normalmente*.
14 tosa.
15 diga *"treinta y tres."*
16 diga *"e."*
17 suba ESTAS escaleras.
18 camine sobre ESTO.

Se siente *mareado* (a)?

6.4 GASTRO-INTESTINAL SYSTEM

EXAMEN FÍSICO DEL SISTEMA GASTRO-INTESTINAL

I am going to examine your . . .
1 abdomen*.
2 rectum.

Voy a examinar su . . .

1 estómago (stomach).
2 ano.

Please . . .

1 try and relax.
2 don't cross your legs.

Por favor . . .

1 cálmese.
2 *no* cruce las piernas.

3 inflate your stomach.
4 suck in your stomach.
5 take a deep breath.
6 hold it.
7 relax.
8 cough.
9 lie on your . . .

   a right side.
   b left side.
10 bend your leg.
11 straighten out your other leg.

Please do it again.

3 *infle* el estómago.
4 *meta* el estómago.
5 inspire *fuerte*.
6 *no* saque el aire.
7 descanse.
8 tosa.
9 *acuéstese* sobre su lado . . .
   a derecho.
   b izquierdo.
10 *doble* la pierna.
11 *estire* la otra pierna.

Por favor, otra vez.

6.5 URINARY TRACT

EXAMEN FÍSICO DEL SISTEMA URINARIO

I am going to examine your kidneys

Please . . .

1 sit up.
2 lean forward.
3 remove your underwear.

Does THIS hurt?

Voy a examinarle los *riñones*.

Por favor . . .

1 siéntese.
2 inclínese hacia *adelante*.
3 *quítese* la ropa interior.

Le duele ESTO.

6.6 REPRODUCTIVE SYSTEM

EXAMEN FÍSICO DEL SISTEMA REPRODUCTIVO

I am going to examine . . .
1 your breasts.
2 your pelvis.
3 your penis.
4 your testicles.
5 for hernias.
6 your genitals

Le voy a examinar . . .
1 los senos.
2 la pelvis.
3 el pene.
4 los testículos.
5 si tiene *hernias*.
6 los genitales.

Do you know how to
examine your breasts?
How often do you do it?
It is important that you
examine your breasts every
_____ weeks (months).
Would you like to learn
how?

Please . . .

1 remove your
   underwear.
2 stand up.
3 cough.
4 bear down.
5 slide closer to the edge
   of the table.
6 put your legs up HERE.

7 open your legs more.
8 relax your muscles.
9 calm yourself.
10 put your arms like
   THIS.

Sabre cómo examinarse sus
senos?
Con qué *frecuencia* lo hace?
Es *importante* que usted se
examine los senos cada
_____ semanas (meses).
Le gustaría *aprender* cómo
hacerlo?

Por favor . . .

1 *quítese* su ropa interior.

2 *levántese.*
3 *tosa.*
4 *puje.*
5 *acérquese* al borde de
   la mesa.
6 *ponga* las piernas
   AQUÍ.
7 *abra* más las piernas.
8 *relaje* los músculos.
9 *cálmese.*
10 *ponga* los brazos ASÍ.

6.7 ENDOCRINE SYSTEM

Please swallow.
Again.

EXAMEN FÍSICO DEL SISTEMA ENDÓCRINO

Trague, por favor.
Otra vez.

6.8 MUSCULO-SKELETAL SYSTEM

Please . . .

1 push against my hand as
  hard as you can.

EXAMEN FÍSICO DEL SISTEMA MÚSCULO-ESQUELÉTICO

Por favor . . .

1 *empuje* fuerte mi mano.

2 squeeze my fingers as hard as you can.

2 *apriete* fuerte mis dedos.

3 don't let me move your . . .
  a head.
  b arm.
  c leg.

3 *no* me deje mover su . . .
  a cabeza.
  b brazo.
  c pierna.

4 raise your . . .
  a arm.
  b leg.

4 levante . . .
  a el brazo.
  b la pierna.

5 relax and let me move your . . .
  a arm.
  b leg.

5 *relájese* y déjeme moverle . . .
  a el brazo.
  b la pierna.

6 repeat THIS same motion.

6 repita ESTE mismo movimiento.

6.9 NERVOUS SYSTEM

EXAMEN FÍSICO DEL SISTEMA NERVIOSO

6.9.1 Mental Status Examination[1]

Examen del Estado Mental[1]

What is your name?
How old are you?
When were you born?
Where are you?
Why are you here?
Who am I?

Cómo se *llama*?
Cuántos años tiene?
En qué *fecha* nació?
Qué lugar es *éste*?
Por qué está aquí?
Quién soy?

What . . .

Qué . . .

1 day is this?
2 month is this?
3 year is this?

1 día es *hoy*?
2 mes es *éste*?
3 año es *éste*?

How much is _____ times _____?

Cuánto es _____ por _____?

What did you eat for breakfast?

Qué desayunó?

Who is the President of the United States?

Quién es el presidente de los Estados Unidos?

[1]For additional questions on memory and recall see page 126–127.

6.9.2 Cranial Nerves[2]

Does THIS smell like . . .
1 cinnamon?
2 clove?
3 mint?
4 alcohol?
5 tobacco?

Don't let me open your . . .

1 mouth.
2 eyes.

Please . . .

1 smile.
2 whistle.
3 try to close your eyes.
4 shrug your shoulders.
5 don't let me move your head.
6 stick out your tongue.
7 move it from side to side.

6.9.3 Sensory

Close your eyes.
Tell me when you feel SOMETHING.
Where do you feel IT?

Please tell me if THIS is . . .

1 hot.
2 cold.
3 like a prick.
4 like a tap.
5 moving . . .
  a upward.
  b downward.

Nervios Craneales[2]

Huele ESTO a . . .
1 canela?
2 clavo?
3 menta?
4 alcohol?
5 tabaco?

No me deje abrir . . .

1 Su boca.
2 sus ojos.

Por favor . . .

1 sonría.
2 silbe.
3 *intente* cerrar los ojos.
4 levánte sus hombros.
5 *no* me deje mover su cabeza.
6 saque la lengua.
7 *muévala* de lado a lado.

Sensibilidad

Cierre los ojos.
Dígame cuando sienta ALGO.
Dónde LO siente?

Siente ESTO . . .

1 caliente.
2 frío.
3 como un *pinchazo*.
4 como un *toquecito*.
5 moviéndose . . .
  a hacia arriba.
  b hacia abajo.

[2]For cranial nerves II, III, IV, VI, VIII, and IX see *Head and Neck* (pp. 61–62).

6.9.4 *Motor*

Please . . .

1 relax.
2 relax your . . .
  a arm.
  b leg.
  c foot.
  d wrist.
3 put your hands like THIS.
4 pull as hard as you can.

6.9.5 **Coordination**

Please . . .

1 close your eyes.
2 keep them shut.
3 stand up with your feet together.
4 hold your arms out straight.
5 walk heel to toe (LIKE THIS).
6 touch my finger with your finger and then touch your nose.
7 put your heel on your ankle.
8 run your heel up and down your leg.

Do IT faster.
Do IT with the other . . .

1 hand.
2 leg.

Movilidad

Por favor . . .

1 cálmese.
2 relaje . . .
  a el brazo.
  b la pierna.
  c el pie.
  d la muñeca.
3 ponga las manos ASÍ.
4 haga *fuerza*.

Coordinación

Por favor . . .

1 *cierre* los ojos.
2 manténgalos *cerrados*.
3 párese con los pies *juntos*.
4 extienda sus brazos *al frente*.
5 camine con un pie delante del otro (ASÍ).
6 *toque* mi dedo con su dedo y luego toque su nariz.
7 *tóquese* el tobillo con el talón.
8 *deslize* el talón sobre su pierna.

HágaLO más rápido.
HágaLO con la otra . . .

1 mano.
2 pierna.

Chapter 7
GENERAL TREATMENT AND FOLLOW-UP

Chapter 7 begins with a section on general therapy. These are patient instructions that do not deal with medications.

Example:

You need to . . .   Necesita . . .

1 stay in bed.   1 *reposar* en cama.
2 avoid excess work.   2 evitar trabajar *demasiado*.
3 take a vacation.   3 tomar vacaciones.

    Section 7.2 contains a list of common laboratory examinations. They are grouped in subsections according to organ systems. Page 153 also contains an index of commonly requested tests in alphabetical order.

In Section 7.3 the technical names of the specialists are given in English. The Spanish translation gives a simplified explanation of each specialty. The literal translation of the Spanish explanation is given in parentheses.

Example:

You need to see . . .

1 a cardiologist*.

Necesita ver un . . .

1 *especialista* en enfermedades de . . . a el corazón (the heart).

7.1 GENERAL THERAPY

You have a problem with your _____.[1]
I don't know what the problem is.
I want you to see a _____ specialist.

You need to . . .

1 have more tests.
2 be hospitalized . . .
   a immediately.
   b in the near future.
3 stay in bed.
4 relax.
5 sleep . . .
   a more.
   b less.
6 avoid getting . . .
   a upset.
   b overtired.
7 get . . .
   a more exercise.
   b less exercise.

TERAPIA GENERAL

Tiene un *problema* con _____.[1]
No sé que es *lo que* le molesta.
Quiero que le *vea* un especialista en enfermedades de _____.

Necesita . . .

1 *más* pruebas.
2 hospitalizarse . . .
   a inmediatamente.
   b próximamente.
3 *reposar* en cama.
4 descansar.
5 dormir . . .
   a más.
   b menos.
6 evitar . . .
   a molestarse.
   b cansarse.
7 hacer . . .
   a *más* ejercicios.
   b *menos* ejercicios.

[1]Throughout this chapter, fill in the blank with the appropriate words.

8	avoid excess work.	8	evitar trabajar *demasiado.*
9	change jobs to one . . .	9	cambiar a un trabajo . . .
	a more active.		a *más* activo.
	b less active.		b *menos* activo.
10	take a vacation.	10	tomar *vacaciones.*
11	enjoy yourself more.	11	divertirse *más.*
12	live in a . . .	12	*vivir* en un clima . . .
	a drier climate.		a *más* seco.
	b more humid climate.		b *más* húmedo.
	c cooler climate.		c *más* frío.
	d warmer climate.		d *más* caliente.
13	eat . . .	13	comer . . .
	a more _____.		a más _____.
	b less _____.		b menos _____.
14	drink . . .	14	beber . . .
	a more _____.		a más _____.
	b less _____.		b menos _____.
15	never . . .	15	no . . .
	a eat _____.		a comer _____.
	b drink _____.		b beber _____.
16	maintain your weight.	16	*mantener* su peso.
17	try to . . .	17	tratar de . . .
	a gain _____ pounds.		a *subir* _____ libras.
	b lose _____ pounds.		b *bajar* _____ *libras.*
	c stop smoking.		c *no* fumar más.
	d stop drinking alcohol.		d *no* beber alcohol.
	e stop using drugs.		e no usar drogas.
18	avoid using your _____.	18	*evitar* el uso de _____.
19	exercise your _____.	19	*hacer* ejercicio con _____.
20	practice THIS.	20	practicar ESTO.
21	keep your feet elevated . . .	21	mantener los pies *elevados* . . .
	a all the time.		a *todo* el tiempo.
	b when you rest.		b cuando *descansa.*
22	avoid straining when you defecate.	22	*evitar* esfuerzos cuando defeca.
23	avoid contact with _____.	23	*evitar* contacto con _____.

24 a cast on your _____.	24 un yeso en su _____.
25 have a transfusion.	25 una transfusión.
26 have an operation . . .	26 una operación . . .
a immediately.	a inmediatamente.
b in the near future.	b próximamente.

Don't get THIS wet.
You can continue your
sexual activities.
I need your permission to do
THIS procedure.
Please sign THIS permission
sheet.
I want to see you in _____.
Your next appointment
is _____.
Please see the . . .

No se moje ESTO.
Puede *continuar* sus
actividades sexuales.
Necesito su permiso para
hacer ESTE tratamiento.
Por favor, firme ESTA hoja
de autorización.
Quiero verle en _____.
Su *próxima* cita es
_____.
Por favor, *véase* con la . . .

1 nurse.	1 enfermera.
2 receptionist.	2 recepcionista.
3 secretary.	3 secretaria.

7.2 LABORATORY EXAMINATIONS[2]

7.2.1 Head and Neck

You need a . . .

1
  a vision test.
  b hearing test.
  c test for glaucoma.
2
  a throat culture.
  b nose culture.
  c ear culture.
3 test for allergies.

4
  a head x-ray.

EXÁMENES DE LABORATORIO[2]

Cabeza y Cuello

Necesita . . .

1 un examen *especial* . . .
  a de la vista.
  b de los oídos.
  c para glaucoma.
2 un cultivo . . .
  a de la garganta.
  b de la nariz.
  c del oído.
3 una prueba para
  alergias.
4 una radiografía . . .
  a de la cabeza.

[2]See Index of Commonly Requested Tests on page 153 for additional tests.

b neck x-ray.

b del cuello.

7.2.2 Cardiovascular-Respiratory Systems

Sistemas Cardiovascular-Respiratorio

You need . . .

Necesita . . .

1 an EKG.
2 an arteriogram.
3 a cardiac catheterization.

4 a cardioversion.
5 a chest x-ray.

6 a sinus x-ray.

7 an echocardiogram.
8 a test for . . .
   a cholesterol.
   b triglycerides.
   c exercise tolerance.

   d pulmonary functions.

9 a blood test.
10 bronchoscopy.
11 a lung scan.

1 un electrocardiograma.
2 un arteriograma.
3 un *cateterismo* cardíaco.

4 una cardioversión.
5 una *radiografía* del pecho.
6 una *radiografía* del seno.
7 un ecocardiograma.
8 un examen de . . .
   a colesterol.
   b triglicéridos.
   c *tolerancia* al ejercicio.
   d las funciones *pulmonares*.
9 una *prueba* de sangre.
10 una broncoscopía.
11 un centellograma de los pulmones.

7.2.3 Gastrointestinal System

Sistema Gastrointestinal

You need . . .

Necesita . . .

1 an upper GI series.

2 a barium enema.
3 a barium swallow.
4 an endoscopy.
5 a cholecystogram.

1 una *serie* gastrointestinal superior.
2 un enema de *bario*.
3 un trago de *bario*.
4 una endoscopía.
5 un colecistograma.

6 a colonoscopy.	6 una colonoscopía.
7 to have . . .	7 un examen . . .
a a proctoscopy.	a proctoscópico.
b sigmoidoscopy.	b sigmoidoscópico.
c a urine analysis.	c de la orina.
d a stool analysis.	d de las heces.
e a liver function test.	e de la *función* hepática.
8 a liver biopsy.	8 una *biopsia* del hígado.
9 a stool culture.	9 un *cultivo* de *heces*.
10 a liver scan.	10 un *centellograma* del hígado.
11 a blood test.	11 una *prueba* de sangre.
12 an x-ray of _____.	12 una radiografía de _____.
13 a CAT scan.	13 una tomografía computada.
14 an ultrasound.	14 un examen de ondas ultrasónicas.
15 a colangiogram	
a endoscopic.	a endoscopic.
b intravenous.	b introvenosa
16 endoscopic retrograde. cholangiopancreatography (ERCP)	16 colangiopancreatografía retrograda endoscópica

7.2.4 Urinary Tract	*Sistema Urinario*
You need . . .	Necesita . . .
1 an . . .	1 un pielograma . . .
a IVP.	a intravenoso.
b retrograde pyelogram.	b retrógrado.
c excretory pyleogram.	c excretono.
2 a cystoscopy.	2 una cistoscopía.
3 to have a . . .	3 un *análisis* de . . .
a urine analysis.	a la orina.
b renal function test.	b la función de los riñones.
c blood test.	c la sangre.
4 a urine culture.	4 un *cultivo* de orina.
5 a renal biopsy.	5 una biopsia del riñón.

6 an ex-ray of your _____.

7 an ultrasound.
8 a catheter . . .
   a Foley.
   b Tenckckoff.
9 dialysis . . .
   a hemo.
   b peritoneal.

7.2.5 Reproductive System

You need . . .

1 to have . . .
   a a breast examination.
   b a pelvic examination.
   c a prostate examination.
   d a blood test.
2 to have . . .
   a a breast biopsy.
   b a uterine biopsy.
   c a prostatic biopsy.
3 a culture . . .
   a of your vaginal secretions.
   b for *Candida*.
   c for *Trichomonas*.
   d for gonorrhea.
   e for syphilis.
   f for herpes.
   g for Chlamydiae.
4 a mammogram.
5 a pap smear.
6 a rectal examination.
7 a semen analysis.
8 a pregnancy test.

9 a laparoscopy.
10 an x-ray of your _____.

6 una *radiografía de* _____.

7 una ultrasonografía.
8 un cáteter . . .
   a Foley.
   b Tenckckoff.
9 diálisis . . .
   a hemo.
   b peritoneal.

Sistema Reproductivo

Necesita . . .

1 un examen de . . .
   a los senos.
   b la pelvis.
   c la próstata.
   d la sangre.
2 una biopsia de . . .
   a los senos.
   b el utero.
   c la próstata.
3 un cultivo . . .
   a de las secreciones *vaginales*.
   b para *Cándida*.
   c para *Tricomonas*.
   d para gonorrea.
   e para sífilis.
   f para herpes.
   g para Chlamydiae.
4 una mamografía.
5 un papanicolau.
6 un tacto *rectal*.
7 un análisis del *semen*.
8 una prueba para el embarazo.

9 una laparoscopia.
10 una radiografía de _____.

7.2.6 Endocrine System

You need . . .

1 an analysis of . . .

  a pituitary function.
  b thyroid function.
  c parathyroid function.
  d pancreatic function.
  e adrenal function.
  f ovarian function.
  g testicular function.
2 a glucose tolerance test.

3 an x-ray of your _____.
4 a blood test.
5 a urine analysis.

7.2.7 Hematologic System

You need . . .

1 a peripheral blood smear.
2 a white cell count.

3 a bone marrow biopsy.

4 to have . . .
  a a serum iron analysis.
  b a blood clotting test.

  c an analysis of your hemoglobin.
  d an analysis of your hematocrit.
  e an analysis of your blood type.
  f a urine analysis.
  g a stool analysis.

Sistema Endócrino

Necesita . . .

1 un *análisis* de la función . . .

  a de la pituitaria.
  b de las tiroides.
  c del paratiroides.
  d del páncreas.
  e de los adrenales.
  f de los ovarios.
  g de los testículos.
2 un examen de *tolerancia* a la glucosa.

3 una radiografía de _____.
4 una *prueba* de sangre.
5 un *análisis* de la orina.

Sistema Hematológico

Necesita . . .

1 un frote periférico.
2 un *recuento* de *glóbulos blancos*.

3 una *biopsia* de la médula ósea.

4 un *análisis* . . .
  a del *hierro* en la sangre.
  b de la *coagulación* de la sangre.
  c de la hemoglobina.

  d de la hematocrita.

  e del *tipo* de sangre.

  f de la orina.
  g de las heces.

5   a transfusion . . .
    a blood.
    b platlet.

5   una transfusión . . .
    a de sangre.
    b de plaquetas.

7.2.8 Musculoskeletal System

You need . . .

1   an x-ray of _____.
2   a blood test.
3   a urine analysis.
4   to have a . . .
    a bone biopsy.
    b muscle biopsy.
5   a muscle function test.

6   a joint . . .
    a aspiration.
    b injection.

7   an anthroscopy.
8   a cast.

Sistema Músculo-Esquelético

Necesita . . .

1   una radiografía de _____.
2   una *prueba* de sangre.
3   un *análisis* de la orina.
4   una biopsia de . . .
    a los huesos.
    b los músculos.
5   un examen de la *función muscular*.

6   una . . .
    a *punción* articular.
    b *inyección* intraarticular.

7   una antroscopía.
8   un yeso.

7.2.9 Nervous System

You need . . .

1   an x-ray of your . . .
    a head.
    b neck.
2   an EEG.
3   a brain scan.

4   a cerebral arteriogram.
5   a lumbar puncture.
6   a myelogram.
7   a CAT scan.

Sistema Nervioso

Necesita . . .

1   una radiografía . . .
    a de la cabeza.
    b del cuello.
2   an electroencefalograma.
3   un *centellograma* del cerebro.

4   un arteriograma cerebral.
5   una *punción* lumbar.
6   un mielograma.
7   una tomografía computada.

8 an MRI scan.	8 una imagen por resonancia magnétic.
9 an audiogram.	9 un audiograma.

7.3 SPECIALISTS*

ESPECIALISTAS*

You need to see . . .

Necesita ver un . . .

1 a specialist in . . .

1 *especialista* en enfermedades de . . .? (specialist in diseases of . . .)

  a internal medicine.
  b otolaryngology.

  a los organos internos.
  b los oídos, la nariz, la garganta (ears, nose, throat.)

  c ophthalmology.
  d cardiology.
  e pulmonologist.

  c los ojos (the eyes).
  d el corazón (the heart).
  e los pulmones (the lungs).

  f gastroenterology.

  f el *aparato digestivo* (the GI tract).

  g nephrology.

  g los riñones (the kidneys).

  h gynecology.
  i endocrinology.

  h la mujer (women).
  i las hormonas (the hormones).

  j orthopedics.
  k pediatrics.
  l hematology.
  m neurology.
  n dermatology.
  o geriatrics.
  p dental problems.

  j los huesos (the bones).
  k los niños (children).
  l la sangre (the blood).
  m los nervios (nerves).
  n la piel (skin).
  o los ancianos (elders).
  p los dientes (the teeth).

2 a specialist in . . .

2 especialista en . . . (specialist in . . .)

  a obstetrics.

  a embarazos y partos (pregnancy and delivery).

b oncology.
c radiology.
d psychiatry.

e nutrition.

3 a psychologist.
4 a surgeon.

b cáncer (cancer).
c radiografías (x-rays).
d problemas
  emocionales
  (emotional problems).
e *dietas y nutrición* (diet
  and nutrition).

3 psicólogo.
4 cirujano.

Chapter 8
MEDICAL THERAPY AND PATIENT INSTRUCTIONS

Chapter 8 is devoted to medical therapy and patient instructions about the use of medications. There are two sections. Section 8.1, Instructions about Medicines, has six subsections that contain the vocabulary needed to explain how medicines should be taken, when they should be taken, and how much should be taken. There are phrases covering previous use of medications, instructions about prescriptions, and a list of possible side effects the patient may experience. The section also contains a series of instructions about the storage of medications.

Section 8.1.6 covers special instructions for the symptoms of insulin overdose and insufficiency. These instructions are written in two forms: the first to communicate directly with the patient and the second to explain the symptoms to family members.

Section 8.2 is an index of some seventy therapeutic and pharmacological classes of medications. It is not a list of medicines by generic or trade name. This information is presented so that the health worker may explain to his patient what type of medicine he or she is taking and why he is taking it.

The different therapeutic and pharmacological groups are listed alphabetically in English by their technical names. The Spanish translation is an explanation of what the medicine is designed to do.

Example:

I am going to treat you with . . .   Le voy a *tratar* con . . .

1   an antiarrhythmic agent.

1   una medicina que *mejora el ritmo de su corazón* (a medicine that improves the rhythm of your heart).

In certain instances, more than just the category of medicine is given. This is done so that the health worker can give more complete information to his patient and still present a simple and understandable explanation.

Example:

I am going to treat you with . . .   Voy a tratarle con . . .

1   insulin that is . . .
    a   short-acting.
    b   medium-acting.
    c   long-acting.

1   *insulina de acción* . . .
    a   corta.
    b   mediana.
    c   larga.

For those health workers who wish to give the specific name of a medication to their patient it is best simply to give the name in English. The patient will probably understand since the names are similar in English and in Spanish. (This is more true for the generic names than for the trade names).

8.1 INSTRUCTIONS ABOUT MEDICINES

INSTRUCCIONES SOBRE LAS MEDICINAS

8.1.1 Prescription Instructions

Instrucciones Sobre las Recetas

THIS is a prescription for your medicine.
You can have it filled at any drugstore.
You can renew it
_____ times.
Please call me . . .

ESTA es una receta para su medicina.
La puede comprar en *cualquier* farmacia.
Puede usar la receta
_____ *veces.*
Por favor, llámeme . . .

1 when you need more.
2 if you do not feel better in _____.
3 if you feel worse.
4 if you have any questions.

1 cuando necesite *más.*
2 si no se siente *mejor* dentro de _____.
3 si se siente *peor.*
4 si tiene alguna *pregunta.*

If you have any reactions, stop the medicine at once and call me.

Si tiene *cualquier molestia,* deje de tomar la medicina y llámeme.

8.1.2 Past Use of Medicines

Empleo Anterior de Medicinas

Have you ever taken THIS medicine before?
When?
For what?
How much did you take a day?
For how long?
Did it help?
Did you have any reactions to it?

Ha tomado ESTA medicina antes?
Cuándo?
Para qué?
Qué *cantidad* tomó diariamente?
Por *cuánto* tiempo?
Le *alivió?*
Tuvo alguna *molestia?*

8.1.3 How and When to Use the Medicines

I am going to give you an injection.

Take _____

1 pills every _____ hours.

2 teaspoons of syrup every _____ hours.
3 tablespoons of syrup every _____ hours.

Take them for _____

1 days.
2 weeks.
3 months.

Please take the medicine . . .

1 _____ times a day.
2 before meals.
3 with meals.
4 after meals.
5 before bedtime.
6 before you exercise.
7 when you have _____ .[1]
8 only when you really need it, because it may be habit-forming.

Drops

Put _____ drops in . . .

1 your nose.
2 your mouth.
3 one eye (both eyes).
4 one ear (both ears).

Cómo y Cuándo Usar las Medicinas

Voy a ponerle una *inyección*.

Tome _____

1 *píldoras* cada _____ horas.

2 *cucharaditas* de jarabe cada _____ horas.
3 *cucharadas* de jarabe cada _____ horas.

Tómelas por _____

1 días.
2 semanas.
3 meses.

Por favor, tome la medicina . . .

1 _____ *veces* al día.
2 *antes* de la comida.
3 *con* la comida.
4 *después* de la comida.
5 *antes* de acostarse.
6 *antes* de hacer ejercicos.
7 cuando tenga _____ .[1]
8 *solamente* cuando la necesite mucho porque produce hábito.

Gotas

Ponga _____ gotas en . . .

1 la nariz.
2 la boca.
3 un ojo (ambos ojos).
4 un oído (ambos oídos).

[1]Fill in the blank with the appropriate symptom.

Cream

Apply the cream to the affected area.

Spray

Inhale the spray through your . . .

1   nose.
2   mouth.

Lozenge

Let is dissolve in your mouth.
Let it dissolve under your tongue.
Chew the tablet.

Powder

Mix _____

1   teaspoons of powder with _____ cups of water.
2   tablespoons of powder with _____ cups of water.

Drink it.
Gargle with the mixture.
Soak your _____ with the mixture for _____ minutes.

Injection

1   subcutaneous
2   intramuscular

8.1.4 Common Side Effects

With THIS medicine you may . . .

Crema

Aplique la crema en el *área afectada.*

Spray

Inhale el spray por . . .

1   la nariz.
2   la boca.

Tableta

Deje que se *disuelva* en la boca.
Deje que se disuelva *debajo* de la lengua.
Mastique la tableta.

Polvo

Mezcle _____

1   *cucharaditas* de polvo con _____ tazas de agua.
2   *cucharadas* de polvo con _____ tazas de agua.

Tómela.
Haga gárgaras con la mezcla.
Sumerja su _____ en la mezcla por _____ minutos.

Inyección

1   subcutánea
2   intramuscular

Efectos Colaterales Comunes

Con ESTA medicina puede tener . . .

1	be irritable.	1	irritabilidad.
2	be depressed.	2	depresión.
3	be agitated.	3	agitación.
4	have insomnia.	4	insomnia.
5	be dizzy.	5	mareos.
6	feel weak.	6	debilidad.
7	have blurred vision.	7	vista *nublada*.
8	have double vision.	8	visión *doble*.
9	have ringing in your ears.	9	*zumbido* de oídos.
10	note a bad taste in your mouth.	10	un sabor *desagradable* en la boca.
11	have a dry mouth.	11	*sequedad* de la boca.
12	be nauseated.	12	náusea.
13	be thirsty.	13	sed.
14	be hungry.	14	hambre.
15	lose your appetite.	15	*falta* de apetito.
16	have excess salivation.	16	salivación *excesiva*.
17	have diarrhea.	17	diarrea.
18	be constipated.	18	estreñimiento.
19	have a change in the color of your urine.	19	*cambio* de color de la orina.
20	have a different-smelling urine.	20	un olor *especial* de la orina.
21	have more vaginal secretions.	21	*más* flujo vaginal.
22	have palpitations	22	palpitaciones.
23	have a rash.	23	una erupción.
24	have red spots.	24	*manchas rojas*.

8.1.5 Storage Instructions

Cómo Guardar las Medicinas

Keep THIS medicine . . .

Guarde ESTE medicina . . .

1 at room temperature.
2 in the refrigerator (not in the freezer).
3 out of strong light.

1 a temperatura *ambiente*.
2 en el refrigerador (*no* en el congelador).
3 donde *no* haya mucha luz.

4 in a dry place.	4 en un lugar *seco*.
5 away from heat.	5 *fuera* del calor.
6 away from children.	6 *fuera* del alcance de los niños.

8.1.6 Instructions for the Diabetic and Family

For the Patient

You should always carry . . .

1 your diabetic ID card.

2 candies.

For Family Members

Help the patient . . .

1 follow his (her) diet.
2 remember to take his (her) insulin.

Instrucciones para el Diabético y la Familia

Para el Paciente

Debe llevar *siempre* . . .

1 su *tarjeta* de *diabético* (a).

2 dulces.

Para los Parientes

Ayude al paciente a que . . .

1 *siga* su dieta.
2 *recuerde* usar su insulina.

INSUFFICIENT INSULIN —FOR THE PATIENT

If . . .

1 you *do not use enough* insulin.
2 if you do not follow your diet,

you may . . .

1 be thirsty.
2 have dry skin.
3 feel nauseated.
4 vomit.
5 faint.
6 have a headache.

INSUFICIENTE INSULINA —PARA EL PACIENTE

Si . . .

1 *no se pone suficiente* insulina.
2 *no come* lo indicado,

puede tener . . .

1 *mucha* sed.
2 piel seca.
3 náusea.
4 vómitos.
5 desmayo.
6 dolor de cabeza.

7   breathe deeply or
     rapidly.
8   urinate frequently.

If THIS happens, you
must . . .

1   ask someone for help.
2   call your doctor.
3   have someone take you
     to the hospital.

INSUFFICIENT INSULIN —FOR FAMILY MEMBERS

If you notice _____ [2]

1   assist the patient with his
     (her) instructions.
2   call the doctor.
3   take the patient to the
     hospital.

INSULIN EXCESS— FOR THE PATIENT

If . . .

1   you *use too much*
     insulin,
2   you do not follow your
     diet,
3   you let too much time
     pass without eating after
     taking your insulin,

7   respiraciones *profundas*
     o *rápidas*.
8   necesidad de *orinar con
     más frecuencia*.

Si ESTO le sucede debe . . .

1   *pedir ayuda* a alguien.
2   *llamar* a *su médico*.
3 . pedir que *le lleven al
     hospital*.

INSUFICIENTE INSULINA—PARA LOS PARIENTES

Si nota _____ [2]

1   *ayude* al paciente con
     sus instrucciones.
2   *llame al médico*.
3   *lleve al paciente al
     hospital*.

EXCESO DE INSULINA—PARA EL PACIENTE

Si . . .

1   *se pone demasiada*
     insulina,
2   *no come* lo indicado,

3   *deja pasar mucho
     tiempo sin comer*
     después de ponerse la
     insulina,

[2]Repeat the symptoms listed under Insufficient Insulin—for the Patient.

4 you exercise too much,
5 you work too much,

you may . . .

1 feel hungry.
2 be weak.
3 have cold sweats.
4 have blurred vision.
5 be nervous.
6 be dizzy.
7 feel confused.
8 have a headache.
9 faint.
10 have palpitations.

If THIS happens, you must . . .

1 eat or drink something sweet *immediately.*
2 ask someone for help.
3 call your doctor.
4 have someone take you to the hospital.

INSULIN EXCESS— FOR FAMILY MEMBERS

If you notice _____ [3]

1 assist the patient with his instructions.
2 call the doctor.
3 take the patient to the hospital.

If the patient is . . .

1 convulsing
2 unconscious

4 hace ejercicio *excesivo,*
5 trabaja *demasiado,*

puede tener . . .

1 hambre.
2 debilidad.
3 sudor *frío.*
4 visión *nublada.*
5 nerviosismo.
6 mareos.
7 confusión.
8 *dolor* de cabeza.
9 desmayos.
10 palpitaciónes.

Si ESTO le sucede, debe . . .

1 comer o beber algo dulce *inmediatamente.*
2 *pedir ayuda* de alguien.
3 *llamar a su médico.*
4 *pedir que le lleve al hospital.*

EXCESO DE IN- SULINA—PARA LOS PARIENTES

Si nota _____ [3]

1 *ayude* al paciente con sus instrucciones.
2 *llame a su médico.*
3 *lleve al paciente al hospital.*

Si el paciente está . . .

1 convulsionando (a)
2 inconciente

[3]Repeat the symptoms listed under Insulin Excess—for the Patient.

NEVER give him (her) anything to eat or drink.	NUNCA le de nada de comer o beber.

8.2 INDEX OF THERA-PEUTIC GROUPS

INDICE DE GRUPOS TERAPEUTICOS

I am going to treat you with a medicine for your illness.	Voy a traterle con una medicina para mejorar su enfermedad.
I am going to treat you with . . . analgesic that is . . .	Le voy a trater con . . . una medicina *para el dolor que* . . . (a medicine for pain that . . .)
1 habit-forming. 2 not habit-forming.	1 puede *producir* hábito. 2 no *produce* hábito.
anesthetic that is . . .	un anestésico . . .
1 local. 2 general.	1 local. 2 general.
antacid	un antiácido
antialcohol agent	una medicina que le ayudará a *dejar de tomar alcohol* (a medicine that will help you stop drinking alcohol)
antiallergen[4]	una medicina *para las alergias*[4]
antiamebic agent	una medicina *para las amebas*
antianginal agent	una medicina *para el dolor del pecho* (a medicine for chest pain)
antiarrhythmic agent	una medicina *para mejorar el ritmo de su corazón* (a medicine that improves the rhythm of your heart)

[4]If no English translation is given in parentheses, then the Spanish phrase is just an explanation of what the drug does:
antiallergen . . . medicine against allergies.
antidiarrheal . . . medicine against diarrhea.

antiarthritic agent	una medicina *para el reumatismo*
antibiotic	antibiótico
anticancer agent	una medicina *para el cáncer*
anticoagulant	una medicina que *evita la formación* de *coágulos*
anticonvulsant	una medicina *para las convulsiones*
antidepressant	una medicina *para la depresión*
antidiarrheal	una medicina *para la diarrea*
antiemetic	una medicina *para los vómitos* (a medicine for vomiting)
antifungal agent	una medicina *para la infección* por *hongos*
antigout agent	una medicina *para la gota*
antihelminthic	una medicina *para las lombrices* (a medicine for worms)
antihemorrhagic agent	una medicina que *evita la hemorragia*
antihistamine	un *antihistamínico*
antihyperlipemic agent	una medicina *para bajar . . .* (a medicine that lowers . . .)

    1 el colesterol
       (cholesterol)
    2 los triglicéridos
       (triglycerides)

antihypertensive agent	una medicina *para bajar su presión* (a medicine that lowers blood pressure)
anti-flammatory agent	una medicina *para la inflamación*
antimalarial agent	una medicina *para la malaria*

antimanic agent	una medicina *para equilibrar* su estado *emocional* (a medicine to balance your emotional state)
anti-motion-sickness agent	una medicina *para* . . . (a medicine for . . .)

1 mareo (dizziness)
2 vértigo (vertigo)

antinauseant	una medicina *para la náusea*
antiparkinson agent	una medicina *para su temblor* (a medicine for your tremor)
antipsychotic agent	una medicina *para modificar su estado mental* (a medicine to modify your mental state)
antipyretic agent	una medicina *para bajar la fiebre* (a medicine that lowers fever)
antiseptic	antiséptico
antispasmodic	una medicina *para aliviar los espasmos*
antithyroid agent	una medicina *para bajar la función de la tiroide* (a medicine that lowers thyroid function)
antituberculous agent	una medicina *para tuberculosis*
antitussive agent	una medicina *para la tos* . . . (a cough medicine . . .)

1 with codeine
2 without codeine

1 *con codeina*
2 *sin codeina*

antiviral agent	una medicina *para las infecciones virales*
appetite depressant	una medicina *para quitar el apetito*
appetite stimulant	una medicina *para estimular el apetito*

bronchodilator	una medicina *para respirar más fácilmente* (a medicine that helps you breathe more easily)
decongestant	un descongestionante
digestant	una medicina *para mejorar la digestión* (a medicine that improves digestion)
digitalis	una medicina *para mejorar la función del corazón* (a medicine that improves the function of your heart)
diuretic	una medicina *para orinar más* (a medicine that makes you urinate more)
emetic	una medicina *para vomitar* (a medicine that makes you vomit)
fertility agent	una medicina que le *ayudará a tener hijos* (a medicine that helps you have children)
hematinic	una medicina *para las anemias* (a medicine that improves anemias)
hematopoietic	una medicina *para producir más sangre* (a medicine that produces more blood)
insulin that is . . .	*insulina de acción . . .*

1   short-acting
2   medium-acting
3   long-acting

1   corta
2   mediana
3   larga

laxative	un laxante
muscle relaxant	una medicina que *relaja los músculos*

oral contraceptive	un *anticonceptivo oral*
oral hypoglycemic	una medicina *para la diabetes* (a medicine for diabetes)
oxytocic	una medicina que *aumenta las contracciones del útero* (a medicine that increases uterine contractions)
sedative	un sedante
steroids . . .	esteroides . . .

1 androgens

2 corticosteroid that is . . .
   a topical
   b oral
   c injectable

3 estrogens

1 *hormonas masculinas* (male hormones)

2 corticoesteroides . . .
   a tópicos
   b orales
   c inyectables

3 *hormonas femeninas* (female hormones)

thyroid drug	una medicina *para aumentar la función del tiroides* (a medicine that increases thyroid function)
tranquilizer	un tranquilizante
vaccine for _____ [5]	una *vacuna* para _____ [5]
vasodilator that is . . .	una medicina *para mejorar le circulación* . . . (a medicine that improves circulation of . . .)

1 general
2 coronary
3 cerebral

vitamins

1 del cuerpo (the body)
2 del corazón
3 del cerebro

vitaminas

---

[5]Fill in the blank with the appropriate vaccine.

Chapter 9
CONTRACEPTION AND PATIENT INSTRUCTION

This chapter contains five sections. Each one is devoted to instructions for the use of a specific method of contraception. This topic is complicated in any language and, unfortunately, the instructions in Spanish are also long. Whenever possible, the instructions are simplified into a series of phrases. Many of the instructions have been left open-ended so that the health worker may substitute his or her preferred instruction.

Example:

Don't douche for _____ hours after intercourse.[1]	*No* emplee duchas vaginales hasta después de _____ horas de sus relaciones.[1]
Do you presently use contraception?	Usa anticonceptivos *actualmente?*
Do you use . . .	Usa . . .

[1]Throughout this chapter, fill in the blank with your own specific instructions.

1 the pill?	1 la *píldora anticon-ceptiva*?
2 the diaphragm?	2 el *diafragma*?
3 an IUD?	3 el *dispositivo intrauterino*?
4 foam?	4 espuma?
5 vaginal tablets?	5 *tabletas vaginales*?
6 condoms?	6 *preservativos* (condones)?
7 the rhythm method?	7 el *método del ritmo*?
8 the method of withdrawal?	8 el *método de retirarse antes de eyacular*?
9 abstinence?	9 *abstinencia*?

Have you had a . . .

Le han operado de . . .

1 tubal ligation?	1 *ligadura de trompas*?
2 vasectomy?	2 vasectomía?

Would you like to have . . .

Le gustaría tener . . .

1 a tubal ligation?	1 una *ligadura de trompas*?
2 a vasectomy?	2 una vasectomía?

Are you satisfied with your present method of contraception?

Está *satisfecho* (a) con su método actual?

9.1 INSTRUCTIONS FOR THE BIRTH CONTROL PILL

INSTRUCCIONES PARA LA PILDORA ANTICONCEPTIVA

It is important to follow all the instructions when taking the pill.
Take the pill at the same time each day.

Es importante seguir *todas* las instrucciones cuando usa la píldora.
Tome la píldora a la *misma hora cada día.*

It can be in the . . .

Puede ser por la . . .

1 morning.	1 mañana.
2 evening.	2 noche.

If you forget to take a pill, you must take it before ＿＿＿ hours have passed. Then take the next pill at the usual hour.

Si *se olvida* tomar una píldora, debe tomarla *antes de que pasen* ＿＿＿ horas. Luego, tome la *próxima* píldora *a la hora acostumbrada*.

With the pill you may . . .

Con la píldora *quizá* . . .

1 gain weight.
2 have . . .
  a enlarged breasts.
  b tender breasts.
3 get headaches.
4 become irritable.
5 have an increased libido.

6 have a decreased libido.

1 *subirá* de peso.
2 *tendrá senos* . . .
  a *más* grandes.
  b *dolorosos*.
3 *tendrá dolor de cabeza*.
4 *estará más irritable*.
5 *aumentarán* sus deseos sexuales.
6 *disminuirán* sus deseos sexuales.

There are three types of pills.

Hay *tres clases* de píldoras.

You have the package of . . .

Usted tiene el paquete de . . .

1 21.
2 28.
3 20.

1 veintiuno.
2 veintiocho.
3 veinte.

Package of 21

Paquete de Veintiuno

1 Take the first pill on the fifth day of your period.

1 Tome la *primera píldora* en el *quinto día* de su regla.

2 Day 1 of your period is the first day you bleed.

2 El *primer día* de su regla es *el primer día* que sangra.

3 Take the pills daily for 3 weeks.

3 Tome las píldoras diariamente *durante tres semanas*.

4 Then stop for 7 days.

4 Luego para *durante siete días*.

5 Your period will come on the second or third day

5 Su regla vendrá el *segundo o tercer día*

after you finish the
package.

6 Begin the next package
on the same day of the
week that you finished
the other pack.

7 If your period does not
start, begin the next pack
as indicated.

Package of 28

1 Take the first pill on the
fifth day of your period.

2 Take THESE for 3
weeks.

3 Take THESE daily for
the next 7 days.

4 On the eighth day begin
a new pack.

5 Your period will begin on
the second or third day
after you begin the last
row of pills (THESE
taken for 7 days).

6 You must take a pill
every day.

7 If your period does not
start, begin the next pack
as indicated.

Package of 20

1 Take the first pill on the
fifth day of your period.

---

después de terminar el
paquete.

6 Empiece el próximo
paquete *el mismo día* de
la semana en que
terminó el otro paquete.

7 Si su regla no viene,
continúe con el próximo
paquete como está
señalado.

Paquete de Veintiocho

1 Tome la *primera
píldora* en *el quinto día*
de su regla.

2 Tome ÉSTAS durante
tres semanas.

3 Tome ÉSTAS
diariamente durante los
próximos siete días.

4 Al *octavo día* empiece
un nuevo paquete.

5 Su regla vendrá el
*segundo o tercer día
después de empezar la
última fila* de píldoras
(*LAS* que tome durante
los siete días).

6 Hay que tomar una
píldora *cada día*.

7 Si su regla no viene,
continúe con el próximo
paquete como está
señalado.

Paquete de Veinte

1 Tome la *primera píldora*
en *el quinto día* de su
regla.

2   Take a pill daily for 20 days.

3   Then stop for 6 days.

4   Your period will come on the second or third day after you stop taking the pills.

5   Begin the new pack on the same day of the week that you finished the other pack.

6   If your period does not start, begin the next pack as indicated.

2   Tome una píldora diariamente durante *veinte días*.

3   Luego pare durante seis *días*.

4   Su regla vendrá el *segundo o tercer día después de terminar* las píldoras.

5   *Empiece* el nuevo paquete *el mismo día* de la semana en que *terminó* el otro paquete.

6   Si su regla no viene, *continúe* con el próximo paquete como está señalado.

9.2   INSTRUCTIONS FOR THE DIAPHRAGM

INSTRUCCIONES PARA EL DIAFRAGMA

You can put it in place _____ hours before having intercourse.
Don't forget to put the special cream on the diaphragm before putting it in.
You can remove the diaphragm _____ hours after intercourse.

Puede ponerlo _____ *hora(s) antes* de tener relaciones sexuales.
No se olvide de poner la crema especial en el diafragma *antes* de ponérselo.
Puede *quitarlo* _____ horas *después* de las relaciones.

9.3   INSTRUCTIONS FOR THE CONDOM, FOAM, AND VAGINAL TABLET

INSTRUCCIONES PARA EL PRESERVATIVO, LA ESPUMA Y LA TABLETA VAGINAL

When used alone . . .

Cuando se usa *solo* (a) . . .

1 the condom is not very safe.

2 foam is not very safe.

3 the vaginal tablet is not very safe.

But it is better than nothing at all.

It is better to use . . .

1 foam with a condom.

2 vaginal tablet with a condom.

Insert the . . .

1 foam _____ hour(s) before intercourse.
2 vaginal tablet _____ hour(s) before intercourse.

The man should wear the condom whenever he enters the vagina, not only during intercourse.

Don't douche for _____ hours after intercourse.
It inactivates the effects of the foam and vaginal tablet.

1 el preservativo, (el condón), *no es muy seguro.*

2 la espuma *no es muy segura.*

3 la tableta vaginal *no es muy segura.*

Pero *es mejor* que no usar nada.

Es *mejor* usar . . .

1 la espuma *con un preservativo (un condón.)*
2 la tableta vaginal *con un preservativo (un condón.)*

Póngase . . .

1 la espuma _____ *hora*(s) *antes* del acto sexual.
2 la tableta vaginal _____ *hora*(s) *antes* del acto sexual.

El hombre *debe* usar el preservativo *cada vez* que el pene tiene contacto con la vagina, *no sólo durante* el verdadero acto sexual.
No emplee duchas vaginales *hasta después de* _____ *horas* de sus relaciones.
Inactiva los efectos de la espuma y de la tableta vaginal.

9.4 INSTRUCTIONS FOR THE IUD

Would you like to use an IUD?
I can fit one for you.
When the IUD is in its proper place, the string will always be the same length.
You can check the length by inserting your finger.
Try IT now.

INSTRUCCIONES PARA EL DISPOSITIVO INTRAUTERINO

Le gustaría usar el *dispositivo intrauterino?*
Puedo *colocarle* uno.
Cuando está bien colocado *el hilo siempre tendrá el mismo largo.*
Puede *comprobarlo* introduciendo el dedo.
HágaLO ahora.

9.5 INSTRUCTIONS FOR THE RHYTHM METHOD

This method is most advisable for a woman who has very regular periods.
You can have intercourse _____ days before your period begins and _____ days after the last day of your period.
You should not have intercourse any other time unless you can use another type of contraception.

INSTRUCCIONES PARA EL MÉTODO DE RITMO

Este método es aconsejable a las mujeres que tienen su *regla puntualmente.*
Puede tener relaciones sexuales _____ días *antes de que* comience la regla y _____ días *después del último día* de la regla.
No se debe tener relaciones los demás días, a *menos que* se emplee *otro método de anticoncepción.*

Chapter 10
PREGNANCY AND DELIVERY

The three sections of this chapter cover history of past pregnancies and deliveries, present pregnancy, and present delivery. The questions and instructions are self-explanatory.

10.1 HISTORY OF PAST PREGNANCIES AND DELIVERIES

How many times have you been pregnant?
How many children do you have?
Did you breast-feed them?

Have you ever had . . .

1 babies that were . . .
   a large?
   b small?
   c premature?

HISTORIA DE PARTOS Y EMBARAZOS ANTERIORES

Cuántas veces ha estado embarazada?
Cuántos hijos tiene?

Les dió el pecho?

Ha tenido . . .

1 niños . . .
   a grandes?
   b pequeños?
   c prematuros?

d congenitally malformed?

2 multiple births . . .

a twins?
b more than two?

3 a forceps delivery?

4 a cesarean?

5 a child that was born . . .
a feet first?
b with the cord around the neck?

6 a child that was born dead?

7 a child that died shortly after birth?

8 problems with the placenta?

9 a postpartum hemorrhage?

10 a miscarriage

11 an abortion?

How many weeks pregnant were you when you had . . .

1 the abortion?
2 the miscarriage?

How long was your labor with the . . .

1 first child?
2 other children?

How much did your children weigh?

---

d con *defectos* de *nacimiento*?

2 nacimientos múltiples . . .

a gemelos (as)?
b *más* de dos?

3 un parto con *forceps*?

4 una cesárea?

5 un niño que haya nacido . . .
a *de pies*?
b con el cordón *alrededor del cuello*?

6 un niño que haya nacido *muerto*?

7 un niño que haya *muerto poco después de nacer*?

8 algún *problema* con la *placenta*?

9 una *hemorragia después* del parto?

10 un aborto *espontáneo*?

11 un aborto *provocado*?

Cuántas semanas de embarazo tenía cuando tuvo el aborto . . .

1 provocado?
2 espontáneo?

Cuánto le duró el trabajo de parto con . . .

1 su *primer* niño?
2 sus *otros* niños?

Cuánto pesaron sus niños?

10.2 PRESENT PREGNANCY

EMBARAZO ACTUAL

I am going to examine you.
What is the date of your last period?

Le voy a *examinar*.
Cuándo fue su *última* regla?

Do you have OR have you had . . .

Tiene O ha tenido . . .

1	anxiety?	1	ansiedad?
2	depression?	2	depresión?
3	irritability?	3	irritabilidad?
4	sleepiness?	4	sueño?
5	insomnia?	5	insomnio?
6	headaches?	6	*dolores* de cabeza?
7	vision problems?	7	molestias de la *vista*?
8	convulsions?	8	convulsiones?
9	nausea?	9	náusea?
10	vomiting?	10	vómitos?
11	constipation?	11	estreñimiento?
12	loss of appetite?	12	*pérdida* de apetito?
13	craving for special foods?	13	antojos?
14	urinary problems?	14	molestias *urinarias*?
15	a lot of vaginal secretions?	15	*mucho* flujo vaginal?
16	tiredness?	16	cansancio?
17	low back pain?	17	dolor de la espalda?
18	swelling of your feet?	18	*hinchazón* en los pies?
19	varicose veins?	19	várices?
20	hemorrhoids?	20	hemorroides?
21	difficulty in breathing?	21	*dificultad* para respirar?
22	high blood pressure?	22	*presión alta*?

You are _____ weeks pregnant.
Was this a planned pregnancy?

Usted tiene _____ semanas de embarazo.
Estaba *planeado* este embarazo?

Do you want to . . .

1 continue with the
   pregnancy?
2 have an abortion?

Do you want to breast-feed
this child?
Do you have any hereditary
diseases?

Quiere . . .

1 *seguir* con el embarazo?

2 tener un aborto
   provocado?

Quiere darle de *mamar* a
este niño?
Tiene alguna enfermedad
hereditaria?

10.3 PRESENT DELIVERY

PARTO ACTUAL

How close together are the
pains?
How long do they last?

Do you know if . . .

1 a lot of water has come
   out?
2 blood has come out?

I am going to examine you.
You are _____ centimeters
dilated.
Do you need to urinate?

I am going to . . .

1 shave you.
2 clean you.
3 give you an enema.

You will have to . . .

1 wait patiently.

2 tell me when you have
   a pain.
3 slide closer to the edge
   of the table.

Cada cuánto le vienen los
dolores?
Cuánto le duran?

Sabe si . . .

1 ha salido *mucha* agua?

2 ha salido *sangre*?

Le voy a *examinar*.
Tiene _____ centímetros *de
cuello*.
Tiene deseos de *orinar*?

Voy a . . .

1 rasurarle.
2 limpiarle.
3 darle un *enema*.

Tendrá que . . .

1 esperar
   tranquilamente.
2 avisarme cuando tenga
   un *dolor*.
3 acercarse *al borde* de la
   mesa.

4   put your legs up HERE.
5   relax your muscles.
6   calm yourself.
7   breathe slowly through
    your mouth.
8   pant.
9   push only when you
    are told.
10 conserve your strength.
11 rest between pains.

12 have an episiotomy.
13 have stitches.

It is a . . .

1   boy.
2   girl.

He (she) weighs
_____ pounds and
_____ ounces.
He (she) is healthy.
Would you like to see your
baby?

4   poner las piernas AQUÍ.
5   *relajar* sus músculos.
6   calmarse.
7   respirar *lentamente* por
    la boca.
8   jadear.
9   empujar solo cuando le
    diga.
10 *conservar* su fuerza.
11 *descansar* cuando no
    tenga dolor.

12 tener una *episiotomía*.
13 tener *puntos*.

Es . . .

1   un niño.
2   una niña.

Pesa _____ *libras* y
_____ onzas.

Es sano (a).
Le gustaría *noital* a su niño
(a)?

Chapter 11
POISONING AND PATIENT INSTRUCTION

This chapter is designed to aid the health worker in cases of intoxication. It contains a list of the more common poisonous agents, immediate instructions for the patient or other party to follow, and a list of general symptoms associated with the various intoxicants.

The text is written in two styles. The first is a set of instructions directed to a third party. For example, a parent calls or brings the child to the hospital because she suspects he (she) has swallowed a poison. The second style is the same set of instructions directed to the patient him- or herself.

The chapter ends with general instructions designed to explain how to help avoid future problems of this nature.

11.1 COMMON INTOXICANTS

What did he (she, you) swallow?
[I don't know.][1]
[I think it is . . .

1 a medicine . . .
   a aspirin.
   b amphetamines.
   c barbiturates.
   d tranquilizers.
   e antiallergen.
   f cough syrup.
   g contraceptives.
   h antiseptics.
2 alcohol.
3 a cleaning agent . . .
   a Clorox.
   b furniture polish.

   c a disinfectant.
   d a detergent.
4 an insecticide.
5 a hair dye.
6 lead from . . .
   a paint.
   b mental toys.
   c batteries.
7 a plant.
8 a mushroom.
9 spoiled food . . .
   a milk and milk
       products.
   b canned goods.]

When did he (she, you) swallow it?

INTOXICANTES COMUNES

Qué tomó?

[No sé.][1]
[Creo que es . . .

1 una medicina . . .
   a aspirina.
   b anfetaminas.
   c barbitúricos.
   d tranquilizantes.
   e antialérgenicos.
   f jarabe para la tos.
   g anticonceptivos.
   h antisépticos.
2 alcohol.
3 un líquido *limpiador* . . .
   a cloro.
   b una *cera para
       muebles.*
   c un desinfectante.
   d un detergente.
4 un insecticida.
5 un *tinte para el pelo.*
6 plomo de . . .
   a pintura.
   b *juguetes* de metal.
   c baterías.
7 una planta.
8 un hongo.
9 una comida *pasada* . . .
   a *leche y derivados.*

   b productos *enlatados.*]

Cuándo lo tragó?

---

[1]The square brackets indicate possible responses by the patient or third party.

How much did he (she, you) swallow?

Call THIS number _____.

Cuánto tragó?

Llame a ESTE número _____.

11.2 INSTRUCTIONS DIRECTED TO A THIRD PARTY

INSTRUCCIONES DIRIGIDAS A OTRA PERSONA

Do the following . . .

1 give him (her) . . .
  a milk.
  b egg whites.
  c vinegar.
  d strong tea.
  e black coffee.
  f mineral oil.
  g antacid.
2 induce vomiting with . . .
  a your finger.
  b mustard and water.`
  c salt and water.
3 bring him (her) to the hospital immediately.

Haga lo siguiente . . .

1 déle . . .
  a leche.
  b *clara* de huevos.
  c vinagre.
  d té *fuerte*.
  e café *negro*.
  f aceite *mineral*.
  g antiácido.
2 hágale *vomitar* con . . .
  a su dedo.
  b agua con *mostaza*.
  c agua con *sal*.
3 tráigale al hospital *inmediatamente*.

11.3 INSTRUCTIONS DIRECTED TO THE PATIENT

INSTRUCCIONES DIRIGIDAS AL PACIENTE

Do the following . . .

1 drink . . .
  a milk.
  b egg whites.
  c vinegar.
  d strong tea.
  e black coffee.
  f mineral oil.
  g antacid.

Haga lo siguiente . . .

1 tome . . .
  a leche.
  b *clara* de huevos.
  c vinagre.
  d té *fuerte*.
  e café *negro*.
  f aceite *mineral*.
  g antiácido.

2   induce vomiting with . . .
   a your finger.
   b mustard and water.
   c salt and water.
3   come to the hospital
   immediately.

2   *vomite* con . . .
   a su dedo.
   b agua con *mostaza.*
   c agua *con sal.*
3   venga al hospital
   immediatamente.

11.4 COMMON SYMPTOMS

SÍNTOMAS COMUNES

Does he (Do you) have OR
has he (have you) had . . .

Tiene O Ha tenido . . .

1	dizziness?	1 mareo?
2	irritability?	2 irritabilidad
3	sleepiness?	3 *mucho* sueño?
4	insomnia?	4 insomnia?
5	depression?	5 depresión?
6	excitability?	6 excitación?
7	convulsions?	7 convulsiones?
8	paralysis?	8 parálisis?
9	confusion?	9 confusión *mental?*
10	incoordination?	10 pérdida de coordinacion?
11	constipation?	11 estreñimiento?
12	nausea?	12 náusea?
13	vomiting?	13 vómitos?
14	diarrhea?	14 diarrea?
15	abdominal pain?	15 cólicos abdominales?
16	headache?	16 *dolor* de cabeza?
17	respiratory difficulty?	17 dificultad *respiratoria?*
18	palpitations?	18 palpitaciones?
19	blue fingers?	19 dedos *morados?*
20	blue lips?	20 labios *morados?*
21	small pupils?	21 pupilas *pequeñas?*
22	large pupils?	22 pupilas *grandes?*
23	blurred vision?	23 vista *nublada?*
24	a dry mouth?	24 *sequedad* de la boca?

11.5 INSTRUCTIONS FOR PREVENTION OF FUTURE INTOXICATIONS

ALWAYS keep all medicines and poisons . . .

1   away from children.

2   in a locked cabinet.

3   in a high place.
4   in their original containers.
5   labeled clearly.

NEVER keep medicines and poisions . . .

1   with food.
2   in food containers such as . . .
    a milk bottles.
    b pop bottles.

INSTRUCCIONES PARA LA REVENCIÓN DE INTOXICACIONES FUTURAS

SIEMPRE guarde medicinas y substancias peligrosas . . .

1   donde los niños *no las alcancen.*

2   en un gabinete cerrado *con llave.*

3   en un sitio *alto.*
4   en su caja *original.*

5   con una etiqueta clara.

NUNCA guarde medicinas y substancias peligrosas . . .

1   donde hay *comida.*
2   en un *recipiente* para la comida como . . .
    a botellas de *leche.*
    b botellas de *soda.*

Chapter 12
AIDS AND PATIENT INSTRUCTION

12.1 INFORMATION FOR THE PATIENT

AIDS is an infection caused by a virus.

SIDA es una infección causada por un virus.

The virus is called HIV.

El virus se llame HIV.

HIV is transmitted by blood products and sexual relations.

HIV se transmite por productos de sangre y relaciones sexuales.

HIV weakens the body's defenses to infection.

HIV debelita las defensas del cuerpo contra infección.

It can take years of infection with HIV before one develops AIDS.

Puede estar infectado con HIV por años antes de tener SIDA.

There is a blood test to detect whether you have been infected by the AIDS virus.

Hay un examen de sangre para detectar si usted está infectado por el virus que causa SIDA.

The blood test is not perfect, but it is extremely accurate.

El examen de sangre no es perfecto, pero es muy exacto.

I need your permission to perform this blood test.

Necesito su permiso para hacer este examen de sangre.

The results of the blood test will be kept confidential.

El resultado del examen será confidencial.

Although there is no cure for AIDS at this time, there are many helpful treatments.

Aunque ahora no hay una cura para SIDA, hay muchos tratamientos efectivos.

Patients with AIDS sometimes get infected with viruses, bacteria, or funguses.

Pacientes con SIDA algunas veces sufren de infecciones de viruses, bacterias; u hongos.

PCP, or pneumocystis, is a type of lung infection that many AIDS patients get.

PCP, o pneumocystis, es una infección del pulmón de la cual sufren muchos pacientes con SIDA.

There is inhaled and intravenous medicine for PCP.

Hay medicina inhalada e intravenosa para PCP.

Kaposi's sarcoma is a tumor that some AIDS patients get.

La sarcoma de Kaposi es un tumor del cual sufren algunos pacientes con SIDA.

The lesions of Kaposi's sarcoma can affect the skin, intestines, lungs, or brain.

Las lesiones de la sarcoma de Kaposi se encuentran en la piel, los intestinos, los pulmones, o el cerebro.

There are medical treatments, including chemotherapy, for Kaposi's sarcoma.

Hay tratamientos, incluyendo quimioterapia contra la sarcoma de Kaposi.

You must be careful not to infect your mate with the HIV virus.

Tiene que ser prudente para no infectar a su compañero (a) con el virus de SIDA.

You must use a condom when having intercourse.

Tiene que usar un condón cuando tiene coito.

Friends and family members with whom you are not intimate are not at risk of getting AIDS from you.

Amigos y miembros de la familia con los cuales usted no tiene relaciones íntimas, no tienen peligro de contraer SIDA de usted.

Chapter 13
GERIATRIC EVALUATION

Chapter 13 is devoted to the new specialty of geriatric medicine. The chapter allows you to evaluate the specific functional problems encountered by the geriatric patient. A mini mental status examination is also provided.

13.1 SOCIAL BACKGROUND

DATOS SOCIALES

How old are you?

Cuántos años tiene usted?

Do you live . . .

Vive . . .

1   alone?
2   with family . . .
   a husband (wife)?

1   solo (a)?
2   con familia . . .
   a esposo (a)?

b brother (sister)?	b hermano (a)?
c grandson (granddaughter)?	c nieto (a)?
d nephew (niece)?	d sobrino (a)?
e cousin?	e primo (a)?
f son-in-law (daughter-in-law)?	f yerno (a)?

3 with a friend?

How long have you lived . . .

1 alone?
2 with family?
3 with a friend?

Are you . . .

1 single?
2 married?
3 widowed?
4 divorced?
5 separated?

For how long . . .

1 weeks?
2 months?
3 years?

Do you have family (friends)
near by?

Who is it?

Where do they live?

Do you speak (visit)
with them . . .

1 daily?
2 weekly?
3 monthly?
4 annually?
5 only on holiday?

Who do you call in case of
emergency?

3 con un amigo (a)?

Cuánto tiempo ha vivido . . .

1 solo (a)?
2 con familia?
3 con un amigo (a)?

Es . . .

1 soltero (a)?
2 casado (a)?
3 viudo (a)?
4 divorciado (a)?
5 separado (a)?

Por cuánto tiempo . . .

1 semanas?
2 meses?
3 años?

Tiene familia (amigos)
cerca?

Quién es?

Dónde viven ellos?

Habla (visita) con
ellos . . .

1 cada día?
2 cada semana?
3 cada mes?
4 cada año?
5 solamente días de fiesta?

A quién llama en caso de
emergencia?

What is their telephone number?	Cuál es su número de teléfono?
Do you know the number for emergency?	Sabe el número a llamar en caso de emergencia?
Can you hear the telephone ring?	Puede oir el teléfono cuando suena?
Do you have electricity in your home?	Tiene electricidad en su casa?
Do you drive a car?	Maneja un carro?
Have you had any accidents recently?	Ha tenido un accidente recientemente?
Can you use . . .	Puede utilizar . . .

1   the bus?   1   el autobús?
2   the train?   2   el tren?
3   taxicabs?   3   un taxi?

13.2   SOCIAL HABITS

HÁBITOS SOCIALES

13.2.1   *Alcohol Use*

Uso de Alcohol

Do you drink alcohol . . .   Bebe alcohol . . .

1   daily?   1   cada día?
2   weekly?   2   cada semana?

How much each day . . .   Cuánto bebe al día . . .

1   glass?   1   vaso?
2   bottle?   2   botella?
3   cup?   3   taza?

Do you drink when you are . . .   Bebe cuándo está . . .

1   alone?   1   solo (a)?
2   sad?   2   triste?
3   depressed?   3   deprimido (a)?
4   happy?   4   alegre?
5   in a social situation only?   5   en una reunión social solamente?

Do you think you have a drinking problem?

Cree que tiene problema de alcoholismo?

Would you like help?[1]

Quiere ayuda?[1]

13.2.2 Smoking Habits

Hábitos de Tabaco

Do you smoke or have you ever smoked . . .

Fuma O ha fumado . . .

1 cigarettes?	1 cigarrillos?
2 pipe?	2 pipa?
3 cigars?	3 cigarros?
4 marijuana?	4 marihuana?

How much do you smoke a day?

Cuánto fuma al día?

How long have you been smoking?

Hace cuánto tiempo que fuma?

Have you ever tried to stop?

Ha tratado de dejar de fumar?

Would you like to stop?

Le gustaría dejar de hacerlo?

13.2.3 Sleeping Habits

Hábitos Para Dormir

Do you ever have problems sleeping?

Tiene problemas para dormir?

What time do you get up in the morning?

A qué hora se levanta por la mañana?

Is your sleep . . .

Duerme . . .

1 restful?	1 tranquilo (a)?
2 interrupted?	2 inquieto (a)?

How many hours do you sleep each night?

Cuántas horas duerme cada noche?

Do you take naps during the day?

Toma siestas durante el día?

How many?

Cuántas?

[1]See page 139 for further questions about alcohol use.

How long? | Cuánto tiempo?

Do you take pills or alcohol to sleep? | Toma píldoras o alcohol para dormir?

How long have you done this? | Hace cuánto tiempo que lo hace?

13.3 MEDICAL BACKGROUND

DATOS MEDICOS

How many medications do you take daily? | Cuántas medicinas toma cada día?

Do you have your medicines here with you? | Tiene sus medicinas aquí ahora?

Please show them to me. | Por favor, déjeme verlas.

Have you had vaccination for . . . | Se ha vacunado contra . . .

1 tetanus? | 1 el tétano?
2 pneumococcal pneumonia? | 2 neumonía de neumococo?
3 influenza? | 3 influenza?

Have you had . . . | Ha tenido . . .

1 a mammogram? | 1 una mamografía?
2 sigmoidoscopy? | 2 una sigmoidoscopía?
3 colonoscopy? | 3 una colonoscopía?
4 a gynecologic examination? | 4 un examen ginecológico?

Was the last one within . . . | El último fue hace . . .

1 six months? | 1 seis meses?
2 a year? | 2 un año?
3 three years? | 3 tres años?
4 five years? | 4 cinco años?

Where was it done? | Dónde lo tuvo?

What medical problems do you have? | Qué enfermedades tiene?

1 high blood pressure? | 1 presión alta?

2 hyperlipidemia . . .	2 hiperlipidemia . . .
a high cholesterol?	a colesterol elevado?
b high triglycerides?	b triglicéridos elevados?
3 heart disease?	3 enfermedad del corazón?
4 myocardial infarct?	4 infarto cardíaco?
5 cerebral infarct?	5 derrame cerebral?
6 varicose veins?	6 várices?
7 thrombophlebitis?	7 tromboflebitis?
8 arteriosclerosis?	8 arterioesclerosis?
9 arthritis?	9 artritis?
10 kidney disease?	10 enfermedad de los riñones?
11 diabetes?	11 diabetes?
12 cancer? What type?	12 cáncer? Qué tipo?
13 bronchitis?	13 bronquitis?
14 tuberculosis?	14 tuberculosis?
15 asthma?	15 asma?
16 pneumonia?	16 neumonía?
17 bleeding tendencies?	17 tendencias a sangrar?
18 anemias . . .	18 anemias . . .
a sickel cell?	a células falciformes?
b thalassemia?	b talasemia?
c iron deficiency?	c deficiencia de hierro?
19 convulsions?	19 convulsiones?
20 mental retardation?	20 retraso mental?
21 psychiatric problems?[2]	21 problemas psiquiátricos?[2]
22 emotional problems?	22 problemas emocionales?
23 glaucoma?	23 glaucoma?
24 congenital defects?	24 defectos de nacimiento?
Do you have pain?	Tiene dolor?
Where is the pain?	Dónde está el dolor?
How long have you had it?	Hace cuánto tiempo que lo tiene?

[2]See Chapter 14 for a detailed psychiatric interview.

Did it develop . . .

1 slowly?
2 suddenly?

Is this (Was that) the first time that you have (had) this type of pain?

When was the first time?

How long does (did) the pain last each time?

Is (Was) it . . .

1 severe pain?
2 mild?
3 moderate?
4 sharp?
5 intermittent?
6 constant?
7 boring?
8 colicky?
9 shooting?
10 burning?
11 cramping?
12 pressurelike?

Where is (was) the pain?

Show me with one finger.

Has (Did) the pain changed (change) location?

Where did the pain begin?

Where does (did) it hurt . . .

1 the most?
2 the least?

Does (Did) the pain radiate?

From where to where?

Se inició . . .

1 lentamente?
2 de repente?

Es (Era) la primera vez que le aparece (aparecía)?

Cuándo fue la primera vez?

Cuánto le dura (duraba) cuando le viene (venía)?

Es (Era) un dolor . . .

1 severo?
2 leve?
3 moderado?
4 agudo?
5 intermitente?
6 constante?
7 penetrante?
8 cólico?
9 fulgurante?
10 quemante?
11 como un calambre?
12 opresivo?

Dónde le duele (dolía)?

Señáleme con un dedo.

Ha cambiado (Cambió) de lugar?

Dónde le empezó?

Dónde le duele (dolía) . . .

1 más?
2 menos?

Se corre (corría) el dolor?

Hacia dónde?

Do (Did) you have the pain . . .

1 all the time?
2 in the morning?
3 in the afternoon?
4 at night?
5 before eating?
6 after eating?
7 while eating?
8 when it is (was) cold?

9 when it is (was) hot?

10 when it is (was) humid?

11 when you are (were) . . .
a upset?
b worried?
12 when you exercise (exercised)?
13 when you urinate (urinated) . . .
a at the beginning?
b the whole time?

c at the end?
14 when you defecate (defecated)?
15 when you have (had) sexual relations?
16 when you swallow (swallowed) . . .
a liquids?
b solids?
c both?
17 when you . . .
a stand (stood)?
b sit (sat) down?

Tiene (Tenía) el dolor . . .

1 todo el tiempo?
2 por la mañana?
3 por la tarde?
4 por la noche?
5 antes de comer?
6 después de comer?
7 mientras come (comía)?
8 cuando hace (hacía) frío?

9 cuando hace (hacía) calor?

10 cuando está (estaba) húmedo?

11 cuando está (estaba) . . .
a molesto (a)?
b preocupado (a)?
12 cuando hace (hacía) ejercicio?
13 cuando orina (orinaba) . . .
a al empezar?
b durante todo el tiempo que orina?
c al terminar?
14 cuando evacúa evacuaba?
15 cuando tiene (tenía) relaciones sexuales?
16 cuando traga (tragaba) . . .
a líquidos?
b sólidos?
c ambos?
17 cuando . . .
a está (estaba) de pie?
b está (estaba) sentado (a)?

c lie (lay) down?

c está (estaba) acostado (a)?

d walk (walked)?

d camina (caminaba)?

e climb (climbed) stairs?

e sube (subía) escaleras?

f bend (bent) over?

f se agacha (agachaba)?

Is (Was) there anything that makes (made) the pain . . .

Hay (Había) algo que . . .

1 better?

1 lo alivie (aliviara)?

2 worse?

2 lo aumente (aumentara)?

What is (was) it?

Qué es (era)?

Is (Was) there anything else that accompanies (accompanied) the pain?

Hay (Había) otras molestias que acompañan (acompañaban) el dolor?

Does (Did) the pain go away when you rest (rested)?

Se alivia (aliviaba) el dolor al descansar?

Do (Did) you awake at night from this pain?

Lo despierta (despertaba)?

Do (Did) you take anything for the pain?

Toma (Tomaba) algo para el dolor?

Does (Did) it help?

Lo alivia (aliviaba)?

Does (Did) it make it worse?

Lo aumenta (aumentaba)?

For the pain do you take . . .

Para el dolor toma . . .

1 aspirin?

1 aspirina?

2 nonsteroidal anti-inflammatory drugs?

2 antiinflamatorio no esteroide?

3 narcotic pain medication?

3 narcóticos?

How is your appetite?

Comó está su apetito?

Has your weight . . .

Su peso . . .

1 increased?

1 ha subido?

2 decreased?

2 ha bajado?

3 stayed the same?

3 es igual?

Do you have problems with . . .

Tiene problemas . . .

1	vision?	1	con los ojos?
2	hearing?	2	con los oídos?
3	walking?	3	para caminar?
4	balance?	4	de equilibrio?
5	bowel incontinence?	5	para retener la orina?
6	bladder incontinence?	6	para retener el excremento?

Do you have an interest in sexual activity?

Tiene interés en actividades sexuales?

Do you have sexual intercourse?

Tiene relaciones sexuales?

Do you have OR have you had any problems with . . .

Tiene O ha tenido problems con . . .

1 erection? . . .
  a There is (was) none?
  b Is (Was) it difficult to achieve?
  c Is (Was) it painful?
2 ejaculation? . . .
  a There is (was) none?
  b Is (Was) it difficult to achieve?
  c Is (Was) it premature?
  d Is (Was) it painful?
  e Is (Was) it bloody?
3 orgasm? . . .
  a There is (was) none?
  b Is (Was) it difficult to achieve?
  c Is (Was) it painful?
4 the quantity of genital secretions? . . .
  a Is (Was) it excessive?
  b Is (Was) it too little?

1 la erección?
  a No la tiene (tenía)?
  b Le cuesta (costaba)?
  c Es (Era) dolorosa?
2 la eyaculación? . . .
  a No hay (había)?
  b Le cuesta (costaba)?
  c Es (Era) prematura?
  d Es (Era) dolorosa?
  e Es (Era) con sangre?
3 el orgasmo? . . .
  a No tiene (tenía)?
  b Le cuesta (costaba)?
  c Es (Era) doloroso?
4 la cantidad de secreciones genitales?
  a Es (Era) excesiva?
  b Es (Era) poca?

Are you OR have you been . . .

Sufre O ha sufrido de . . .

1 physically abused?
2 sexually abused?

1 abuso físico?
2 abuso sexual?

13.4 FUNCTIONAL ASSESSMENT

EVALUACION FUNCIONAL

Do you have problems . . .

Tiene problemas . . .

1	getting out of bed by yourself?	1	para levantarse de la cama solo (a)?
2	getting out of a chair by yourself?	2	para levantarse de una silla solo (a)?
3	getting out of a bath or shower by yourself?	3	para salir del baño o la ducha solo (a)?
4	going up and down stairs?	4	para subir o bajar las escaleras solo (a)?
5	getting washed by yourself?	5	para lavarse solo (a)?
6	brushing your teeth?	6	para cepillarse los dientes?
7	getting dressed by yourself?	7	para vestirse solo (a)?
8	with household chores?	8	para hacer tareas de la casa?
9	shopping for yourself?	9	para ir de compras solo (a)?
10	falling down?	10	cayéndose?
11	with fatigue?	11	de cansancio?
12	concentrating?	12	para concentrarse?
13	understanding?	13	para entender?
14	getting lost?	14	perdiéndose?
15	remembering . . .	15	para recordar . . .
	a names?		a nombres?
	b dates?		b datos?
	c phone numbers?		c números de teléfono?
	d directions?		d direcciones?
	e the past?		e el pasado?
16	losing things?	16	perdiendo las cosas?
17	preparing your meals?	17	para preparar sus comidas?
18	eating your meals?	18	par comer solo (a)?

Do you have . . .

Tiene . . .

1	pain with chewing?	1	dolor al masticar?
2	your own teeth?	2	los dientes propios?
3	dentures?	3	dientes postizos?

4 problems with how your dentures fit?
5 trouble with . . .

a solid food?
b liquids?
6 diet changes because of these problems?

Do you pay the . . .

1 rent alone?
2 bills alone?

Does anyone help you?

Who?

4 problemas con los dientes postizos?
5 problemas con la comida . . .

a sólida?
b líquida?
6 cambios en la dieta a causa de estos problemas?

Paga . . .

1 la renta solo (a)?
2 las cuentas solo (a)?

Alguién le ayuda?

Quién es?

13.5 MENTAL AND EMOTIONAL ASSESSMENT

Do you often feel OR have you felt . . .

1 afraid?
2 angry?
3 anxious?
4 bored?
5 depressed?
6 guilty?
7 happy to be alive?
8 hopeless?
9 isolated?
10 lonely?
11 sad?
12 your life is empty?

13 worthless?

Do you prefer to . . .

EVALUACION MENTAL EMOCIA

Se siente O ha sentido . . .

1 asustado?
2 enojado (a)?
3 ansioso (a)?
4 aburrido (a)?
5 deprimido (a)?
6 culpable?
7 feliz de vivir?
8 sin esperanza?
9 aislado (a)?
10 solo (a)?
11 triste?
12 que su vida está vacía?

13 sin valor?

Prefiere . . .

1	stay at home?		1	estar solo (a)?
2	go out?		2	salir?
3	visit with people?		3	visitar a otros?
4	try new things?		4	tratar cosas nuevas?
5	meet new people?		5	conocer nueva gente?

What is the . . .

Cuál es . . .

1	season?		1	la estación del año?
2	day?		2	el día?
3	month?		3	el mes?
4	year?		4	el año?
5	state?		5	el estado?
6	city?		6	la cuidad?

Please repeat these three objects . . .

Por favor repita estas tres cosas . . .

1	house		1	casa
2	car		2	carro
3	book		3	libro

Please remember these 3 objects . . .

Por favor recuerde estas tres cosas . . .

1	house		1	casa
2	car		2	carro
3	book		3	libro

I will ask you to repeat them later.[3]

Más tarde, se las voy a preguntar.[3]

Please tell me the three objects.

Por favor, dígame las tres cosas.

Please subtract 7 from 100 and keep going down by seven.

Por favor, reste cien menos siete y menos siete más.

93	noventa y tres
86	ochenta y seis
79	setenta y nueve
72	setenta y dos
65	sesenta y cinco

[3]The questioner should wait approximately five minutes before asking the patient to recall the three objects.

Please spell the word WORLD backwards.	Por favor, deletree la palabra MUNDO al revés.
Please say the days of the week backwards, starting with Saturday.	Por favor, dígame los días de la semana al revés, comenzando con el sábado?

Saturday	sábado
Friday	viernes
Thursday	jueves
Wednesday	miércoles
Tuesday	martes
Monday	lunes
Sunday	domingo

What are THESE objects . . .	Qué son ESTAS cosas . . .

1 wrist watch?	1 reloj de pulsera?
2 pencil?	2 lápiz?

Please follow these instructions . . .	Por favor, sigua estas instrucciones . . .

1 take this paper in your right hand	1 tome el papel en su mano derecha
2 fold it in half	2 doble el papel por el medio.
3 place it on the floor	3 póngalo en el suelo.
4 point to the . . .	4 señale . . .
a ceiling	a el cielo
b floor	b el piso
c chair	c el asiento

Please . . .	Hágame el favor de . . .

1 read THIS and do what it says. (See Figure 1)	1 leer ÉSTO y hacer lo que dice.

> **HAGA EL FAVOR DE**
> **CERRAR LOS OJOS**
> **(CLOSE YOUR EYES)**

Figure 1

2   write a sentence.
3   copy the drawing.
    (See Figure 2)

2   escribir una frase.
3   copiar este dibujo.

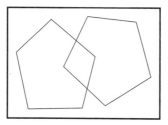

Figure 2

Please . . .

1   draw a large circle.
2   put numbers in the circle
    so that it resembles a clock.

3   have the clock hands show
    11:10.

Por favor . . .

1   dibuje un círculo grande.
2   ponga números en el
    círculo para que parezca
    un reloj.
3   ponga las manos del reloj
    para que diga 11:10.

13.6   LETHALITY ASSESSMENT[4]

EVALUACIÓN DEL INTENTO MORTAL[4]

DO YOU HAVE THOUGHTS ABOUT HARMING YOURSELF?

TIENE PENSAMIENTOS DE HACERSE DAÑO?

DO YOU HAVE PLANS HOW YOU WOULD DO IT?

TIENE IDEAS DE CÓMO LO HARÍA?

DO YOU HAVE ACCESS TO WEAPONS?

TIENE ACCESO A LAS ARMAS?

HAVE YOU ATTEMPTED TO HARM YOURSELF BEFORE?

HA TRATADO DE HACERSE DAÑO ANTES?

---

[4]Questions in bold are considered very important lines of inquiry and affirmative replies should prompt psychiatric referral.

Do you feel . . .	Se siente . . .

1	hopeless?	1	sin esperanza?
2	you would be better off dead?	2	qué sería mejor si estuviera muerto (a)?
3	others would be better off if you were dead?	3	qué sería mejor para los demás si usted estuviera muerto (a)?
4	you have problems controlling impulses?	4	que tiene problemas para controlar sus impulsos?

DO YOU HAVE THOUGHTS ABOUT WANTING TO HARM SOMEONE ELSE?	**TIENE IDEAS DE HACERLE DAÑO A OTROS?**
DO YOU HAVE PLANS ON HOW YOU WOULD HARM THEM?	**TIENE IDEAS DE CÓMO LO HARÍA?**
DO YOU HAVE ACCESS TO THIS PERSON?	**PUEDE ENCONTRAR A ESA PERSONA?**
DO YOU HAVE ACCESS TO WEAPONS?	**TIENE ACCESO A LAS ARMAS?**
HAVE YOU HARMED SOMEONE PREVIOUSLY?	**LE HA HECHO DAÑO A OTRA PERSONA ANTES?**

Have you ever been charged with . . .	Le han acusado de . . .

1	assault?	1	asalto?
2	homicide?	2	homicidio?

Do you have trouble controlling unpleasant feelings, for example, anger, rage?	Tiene problemas para controlar las emociones malas, por ejemplo el enojo?

Chapter 14
THE PSYCHIATRIC INTERVIEW

This chapter provides questions for an indepth psychiatric interview. Questions that are considered to be highly significant areas of inquiry are bold faced and capitalized.

14.1 DEPRESSION

Has your mood been . . .

1   sad?
2   irritable?
3   tearful?

DEPRESIÓN

Su estado de ánimo ha sido . . .

1   triste?
2   irritable?
3   lagrimoso?

Have you felt this way for . . .	Se ha sentido así . . .

1	a few days?	1	pocos días?
2	a week?	2	una semana?
3	two to three weeks?	3	dos o tres semanas?
4	months?	4	meses?
5	as long as you can remember?	5	todo el tiempo que puede recordar?

Do you have interest in activities?	Tiene interés en actividades?
When something good happens, do you feel happy?	Cuando algo bueno occure, se siente feliz?
Have you stopped many of your interests?	Ha dejado de hacer las cosas que le interesan?
Has there been a change in your interest in . . .	Ha cambiado su interés en . . .

1	watching TV?	1	mirar la televisión?
2	music?	2	la música?
3	reading?	3	leer?
4	shopping?	4	ir de compras?
5	socializing?	5	actividades sociales?
6	sex?	6	relaciones sexuales?

Has there been a change in your sleep?	Ha cambiado cómo duerme?
Is it . . .	Duerme . . .

1	increased?	1	más?
2	decreased?	2	menos?

Do you feel tired?	Se siente cansado (a)?
Do you have energy to complete day-to-day tasks?	Tiene energía para completar las tareas diarias?
Do you feel OR have you felt . . .	Se siente O ha sentido . . .

1 slowed down?	1 pesado (a)?
2 restless?	2 inquieto (a)?

Has there been a change
in your . . .

Ha cambiado su . . .

1 appetite?	1 apetito?
2 weight?	2 peso?

Is it . . .

Ha . . .

1 increased?	1 subido?
2 decreased?	2 bajado?

Do you have difficulty . . .

Tiene dificultad para . . .

1 making decisions?	1 hacer deciciones?
2 concentrating on . . .	2 concentrarse en . . .
a activities?	a las actividades?
b conversation?	b la conversación?

Comparing yourself to others,
do you have more problems
with your memory?

Comparándose con los
demás, tiene más
problemas con la memoria?

Do you feel OR have you felt . . .

Siente O ha sentido . . .

1 guilty?	1 culpable?
2 badly about yourself?	2 vergüenza por si mismo?
3 hopeless about your future?	3 sin esperanza para el futuro?
4 worthless as you are?	4 que vale nada?

DO YOU THINK ABOUT DYING?[1]

PIENSA EN LA MUERTE?[1]

DO YOU WISH YOU WERE DYING?

DESEA MORIRSE AHORA?

DO YOU WISH YOU WERE DEAD?

DESEA ESTAR MUERTO (A) AHORA?

DO YOU THINK OF WAYS TO HARM YOURSELF?

PIENSA EN CÓMO HACERSE DAÑO?

---

[1]Questions in bold are considered very important lines of inquiry and affirmative replies should prompt psychiatric referral.

Have you been treated by
a doctor for this problem
before?

Ha recibido tratamiento
médico por este problema
antes?

Have you been hospitalized for
this problem before?

Ha estado hospitalizado
por este problema antes?

14.2   MANIA

MANÍA

Do you feel OR have you felt . . .

Siente O ha sentido . . .

1   happier than usual?
2   **IRRITABLE?**
3   excited?
4   **ON-TOP-OF-THE-
    WORLD?**
5   there was nothing you
    couldn't do?

1   más feliz que lo normal?
2   **IRRITABLE?**
3   excitado (a)?
4   **ENCIMA DEL
    MUNDO?**
5   que puede hacer todo
    lo que quiere sin limites?

Do you have more energy
than usual?

Tiene más energía que lo
normal?

Do you have less need for sleep
lately?

Necesita dormir menos
recientemente?

**HAVE YOU FELT YOUR
THOUGHTS WERE SO
FAST YOU COULDN'T
KEEP UP WITH THEM?**

**HA SENTIDO QUE SUS
PENSAMIENTOS
VIENEN TAN
RAPIDAMENTE QUE
NO PUEDE
CONTROLARLOS?**

Have others commented that
they cannot follow your train of
thought?

Le han dicho otros que no
pueden entender sus ideas
o sus pensamientos?

Have you been more talkative
than usual?

Habla más que lo normal?

**HAVE YOU BEEN TAKING
ON MORE ACTIVITIES
THAN USUAL?**

**ESTÁ HACIENDO MÁS
ACTIVIDADES QUE LO
NORMAL?**

Are you . . .	Está . . .
1 working more?	1 trabajando más?
2 more physically active?	2 haciendo más actividad física?
3 spending more money?	3 gastando más dinero?
4 spending money foolishly?	4 gastando dinero sin pensar?
5 making excessive investments?	5 haciendo inversiones excesivas?
6 more sexually active?	6 participando más en actividades sexuales?

Have others commented that your behavior is excessive?	Le han dicho otros que su comportamiento es excesivo?

Have you felt this way for . . .	Se ha sentido así . . .
1 a few days?	1 pocos días?
2 a week?	2 una semana?
3 two to three weeks?	3 dos o tres semanas?
4 months?	4 meses?
5 as long as you can remember?	5 todo el tiempo que puede recordar?

Have you been treated by a doctor for this problem before?	Ha recibido tratamiento médico por este problema antes?

Have you been hospitalized for this problem before?	Ha estado hospitalizado por este problema antes?

14.3 LETHALITY ASSESSMENT
EVALUACIÓN DEL INTENTO MORTAL

DO YOU HAVE THOUGHTS ABOUT HARMING YOURSELF?

TIENE PENSAMIENTOS DE HACERSE DAÑO?

DO YOU HAVE PLANS ON HOW YOU WOULD DO IT?

TIENE IDEAS DE CÓMO LO HARÍA?

DO YOU HAVE ACCESS TO WEAPONS?	**TIENE ACCESO A LAS ARMAS?**

HAVE YOU ATTEMPTED TO HARM YOURSELF BEFORE?	**HA TRATADO DE HACERSE DAÑO ANTES?**

Do you feel . . .

Se siente . . .

1	hopeless?	1	sin esperanza?
2	you would be better off dead?	2	qué sería mejor si estuviera muerto (a)?
3	others would be better off if you were dead?	3	qué sería mejor para los demás si usted estuviera muerto (a)?
4	you have problems controlling impulses?	4	que tiene problemas para controlar sus impulsos?

DO YOU HAVE THOUGHTS ABOUT WANTING TO HARM SOMEONE ELSE?	**TIENE IDEAS DE HACERLE DAÑO A OTROS?**

DO YOU HAVE PLANS ON HOW YOU WOULD HARM THEM?	**TIENE IDEAS DE CÓMO LO HARÍA?**

DO YOU HAVE ACCESS TO THIS PERSON?	**PUEDE ENCONTRAR A ESTA PERSONA?**

DO YOU HAVE ACCESS TO WEAPONS?	**TIENE ACCESO A LAS ARMAS?**

HAVE YOU HARMED SOMEONE PREVIOUSLY?	**LE HA HECHO DAÑO A OTRA PERSONA ANTES?**

Have you ever been charged with . . .

Le han acusado de . . .

1	assault?	1	asalto?
2	homicide?	2	homicidio?

Do you have trouble controlling unpleasant feelings, for example, anger, rage?

Tiene problemas para controlar las emociones malas, por ejemplo el enojo?

14.4 PSYCHOSIS

PSICOSIS

14.4.1 Delusions

. . . of reference:

Do you feel as if, when the television or radio are on, they are sending messages intended just for you?

Siente que la televisíon or la radio, mandan mensajes solamente para usted?

Does it seem as if others, even those you don't know, are taking special notice of you?

Le parece que otros, incluyendo los extraños, le prestan atención especial?

. . . of grandeur:

Do you feel you have special powers or magical abilities no one else has?

Se siente que tiene abilidades especiales o mágicas que no tienen los demás?

. . . of persecution:

Do you feel others . . .

Se siente que otros . . .

1 are conspiring against you?

1 están conspirando contra usted?

2 are out to get you?
3 may harm you?

2 quieren castigarle?
3 quieren hacerle daño?

. . . of guilt:

Do you feel you have done something so bad that you feel you are being punished?

Se siente que ha hecho algo tan malo que le están castigando por hacerlo?

Do you feel responsible for events going on in the world . . .

Se siente responsable por acciones mundiales . . .

1 war?
2 starvation?

1 las guerras?
2 la inanición?

. . . of control:

Do you feel someone or something is controlling what you do from afar?	Se siente que alguién o algo está controlándole de lejos?

. . . of thought broadcasting:

Do you feel others can hear your thoughts without you saying or doing anything?	Se siente que otros pueden oír sus pensamientos aunque no diga o haga nada?
Do you feel people "read your mind" and know what you are thinking?	Se siente que otra gente puede "leer sus pensamientos" y entender lo que está pensando?

. . . of thought insertion:

Do you feel others can insert thoughts or ideas into your head?	Se siente que otros pueden poner ideas o pensamientos dentro de su cabeza?

. . . of depersonalization:

Does your body feel . . .	Siente su cuerpo . . .

1	strange?	1	extraño?
2	changed?	2	cambiado?
3	disconnected?	3	desconectado?

Do you feel as if you are in a movie, watching yourself go through the motions?	Se siente como si estuviera haciendo un papel en una película, mirándose a si mismo hacer las cosas?

. . . of unreality:

Does the world seem changed to you?	Le parece cambiado el mundo?
Do . . .	Se ven iqual que siempre . . .

1	people	1	la gente?

2	cars	2	los carros?
3	houses	3	las casas?
4	trees	4	los árboles?
5	animals	5	los animales?

appear as they usually do?

14.4.2 Hallucinations

DO YOU EVER SEE THINGS OTHERS WOULD BE UNABLE TO SEE?

VE USTED COSAS QUE OTROS NO PUEDEN VER?

DO YOU EXPERIENCE VISIONS?

TIENE VISIONES?

DO YOU HEAR VOICES OTHERS ARE UNABLE TO HEAR?

OYE USTED VOCES QUE OTROS NO PUEDEN OIR?

DO YOU HEAR VOICES TALKING TO YOU OR ABOUT YOU?

OYE USTED VOCES QUE LE HABLAN O VOCES QUE HABLAN DE USTED?

DO YOU HEAR VOICES TELLING YOU/ COMMANDING YOU TO DO THINGS?

OYE USTED VOCES QUE LE MANDAN A HACER COSAS?

Do you experience smells/odors other people don't notice?

Huele olores que nadie más huele?

Do you experience unusual sensations on your skin?

Siente sensaciónes diferentes en la piel?

Do you experience crawling/ creeping sensations on your skin?

Se siente que algo se arrastra por su piel?

Do you experience unusual tastes in your mouth?

Prueba sabores diferentes en la boca?

Have you felt this way for a long time?

Hace tiempo que se siente así?

Have you been treated by a doctor for this problem before?	Ha recibido tratamiento médico por este problema antes?
Have you been hospitalized for this problem before?	Ha estado hospitalizado por este problema antes?

14.5 ALCOHOL AND DRUG USE

USO DE ALCOHOL Y DROGAS

Do you drink alcohol?	Toma alcohol?
Do you have periods when you get drunk?	Se emborracha?
Do you notice if it takes more for you to get drunk than it had previously?	Nota si tiene que beber más que antes para emborracharse?
When you stop drinking, do you have . . .	Cuando deja de tomar alcohol tiene . . .

1	tremors?	1	temblores?
2	sweating?	2	sudores?
3	nervousness?	3	nerviosismo?
4	difficulty sleeping?	4	dificultad para dormir?
5	nausea?	5	nausea?
6	vomiting?	6	vómitos?

Do you drink . . .   Toma alcohol . . .

1	to stop any of these symptoms?	1	para parar estos síntomas?
2	for longer than you intended?	2	durante más tiempo del que había planeado?
3	more than you intended?	3	en cantidades más grandes de las que había planeado?

Do you spend more time . . .   Pasa más tiempo . . .

1	trying to acquire alcohol?	1	buscando alcohol?
2	drinking?	2	tomando alcohol?
3	hiding your drinking?	3	escondiendo su hábito de alcohol?

4 recovering from drinking episodes?	4 recuperándose de una borrachera?

Because of your drinking have you . . .

Por culpa del alcohol . . .

1 missed work?	1 ha faltado al trabajo?
2 been fired from work?	2 ha perdido el trabajo?
3 been suspended from school?	3 le han suspendido de la escuela?
4 argued with your wife/ husband?	4 ha peleado con su esposa (o)?
5 been separated or divorced?	5 se ha separado o divorciado?
6 spent less time with your family?	6 ha pasado menos tiempo con la familia?
7 been arrested?	7 lo han arrestado?

Have you thought about . . .

Ha pensado en . . .

1 stopping your drinking?	1 dejar el alcohol?
2 controlling your drinking?	2 controlar el alcohol?

Have you been in . . .

Ha participado en . . .

1 detoxification?	1 desintoxicación?
2 rehabilitation?	2 rehabilitación?
3 outpatient treatment?	3 tratamiento ambulatorio?

When did you last drink alcohol?

Cuándo tomó alcohol por última vez?

Do you drink despite . . .

Toma alcohol aunque . . .

1 having medical problems?	1 tiene problemas médicos?
2 your doctor advising against it?	2 su médico recomienda lo contario?

Have you ever had . . .

Ha sufrido de . . .

1 black outs?	1 lagunas mentales?
2 hangovers?	2 resacas?
3 delirium tremens?	3 delirium tremens?

Do you use OR have you ever used . . .

Usa O ha usado . . .

1	marijuna?
2	cocaine?
3	heroin?
4	LSD?
5	PCP?
6	mescaline?
7	amphetamines?
8	Ecstasy?
9	barbiturates?
10	benzodiazepines?

1	marihuana?
2	cocaina?
3	heroína?
4	LSD?
5	PCP?
6	mescalina?
7	anfetamina?
8	Ecstasis?
9	barbitúricos?
10	benzodiacepinas?

14.6 ANXIETY

ANSIEDAD

Do you have times when you feel nervous?

Tiene momentos cuando se siente nervioso (a)?

When you feel nervous, do you . . .

Cuando se siente nervioso (a) sufre de . . .

1	feel shaky or tremble?
2	feel tense, have sore muscles?
3	feel fidgety or can't sit still?
4	get tired easily?
5	have dry mouth?
6	get dizzy or lightheaded?
7	have cold, clammy hands?
8	feel your heart beat fast?
9	feel like you can't catch your breath?
10	feel you can't swallow?
11	have hot flashes/chills?
12	urinate more frequently than usual?
13	have trouble concentrating?
14	jump if you hear sudden noises?

1	temblores?
2	tensión o múculos dolorosos?
3	inquietitude?
4	cansansio?
5	la boca seca?
6	mareos?
7	las manos frías o pegajosas?
8	palpitaciones?
9	falta de aire?
10	dificultad para tragar?
11	calores o escalofríos?
12	orina frequente?
13	poca concentración?
14	sustos con ruídos fuertes?

15 have trouble falling asleep?	15 dificultad para dormir?

When you feel nervous, how long do these periods last?

Cuando se siente nervioso (a), cuánto tiempo dura?

Are these periods brought on by . . .

Estos momentos occuren cuando . . .

1	being around many people?	1	está con mucha gente?
2	being watched by others?	2	otros le miran?
3	being in certain situations . . .	3	está en ciertas situaciones . . .
	a heights?		a las alturas?
	b around animals?		b cerca de animales?
4	being in certain places . . .	4	está en ciertos lugares . . .
	a crowded places?		a sitios que están llenos de gente?
	b long lines?		b colas largas?
	c buses?		c autobuses?
	d trains?		d trenes?
	e planes?		e aviones?
	f large parking lots?		f parques de estacionamiento grandes?

Are you a nervous person?	Está nervioso (a)?
Do you worry often?	Se preocupa mucho?
Do people tell you that you worry too much?	Le dicen que se preocupa demasiado?
Are you bothered by thoughts that play in your head over and over again?	Tiene pensamientos que le occuren repetidas veces en su mente?
Are these thoughts distressing to you?	Le molestan estos pensamientos?
Do you find it hard to control such thoughts?	Le resulta difícil controlar estos pensamientos?
Do you find you must repeat certain activities in order to reduce your distress?	Tiene que repetir ciertas actividades para bajar su angustia?

Do you find you must do things in a particular way or a particular number of times in order to feel relaxed or in order to prevent something bad from happening?

Tiene que hacer las cosas en una manera particular o cierto número de veces para sentirse cómodo (a) o para evitar que algo malo no pase?

If you can't do it the way you like or the number of times you like, do you feel . . .

Si no puede hacerlo como quisiera o el número de veces que quisiera, se siente . . .

1   anxious?
2   distressed?
3   restless?
4   irritable?

1   ansioso (a)?
2   angustiado (a)?
3   inquieto (a)?
4   irritable?

14.7 SOMATOFORM DISORDERS

ENFERMEDADES SOMÁTICAS

Do you feel you have a serious medical condition?

Siente que tiene un problema médico grave?

Have you sought out medical evaluation?

Ha buscado evaluación médica?

Has it been reassuring?

Le ha dado seguridad?

When reassured that nothing is wrong, do you still worry . . .

Cuándo le aseguran de nuevo que todo está bien, todavía se preocupa . . .

1   about your health?
2   that the doctor missed something?

1   por su salud?
2   que el médico le faltaba algo?

Are you bothered by many physical complaints?

Tiene muchas molestias físicas?

Have you had a lot of trouble with . . .

Tiene muchos problemas con . . .

1   vomiting? (when not pregnant)
2   nausea?
3   diarrhea?

1   vómitos? (cuando no está embarazada)
2   náusea?
3   diarrea?

4	back pain?	4	dolor de la espalda?
5	arm pain?	5	dolor del brazo?
6	leg pain?	6	dolor de la pierna?
7	pain with urination?	7	dolor al orinar?
8	difficulty swallowing?	8	dificultad para tragar?
9	losing your voice?	9	pérdida de la voz?
10	going blind for a short while?	10	pérdida de la vista?
11	periods of amnesia?	11	amnesia?

Appendix
GENERAL VOCABULARY

A.1 DAYS, MONTHS, HOLIDAYS

Days of the Week[1]

Monday
Tuesday
Wednesday
Thursday
Friday
Saturday
Sunday

Días de la Semana[1]

lunes
martes
miércoles
jueves
viernes
sábado
domingo

Months of the Year

January
February
March
April
May
June
July
August
September
October

Meses del Año

enero
febrero
marzo
abril
mayo
junio
julio
agosto
septiembre
octubre

[1]In Spanish, days of the week and months of the year are not capitalized.

November	noviembre
December	diciembre
today	hoy
yesterday	ayer
tomorrow	mañana
day before yesterday	anteayer
day after tomorrow	pasado mañana
last year	el año pasado
last month	el mes pasado
last week	la semana pasada
this year	este año
this month	este mes
this week	esta semana
next year	el año próximo
next month	el mes próximo
next week	la semana próxima

Holidays   **Días de Fiesta**

Christmas	Navidad
New Year	Año Nuevo
Valentine's Day	Día de San Valentín
Easter	Pascua
Holy Week	Semana Santa
July 4	Cuatro de julio
Halloween	Día de todos los Santos
birthday	cumpleaños
anniversary	aniversario

A.2 CARDINAL AND ORDINAL NUMBERS

NÚMEROS CARDINALES Y ORDINALES

Cardinal Numbers

1	uno		14	catorce
2	dos		15	quince
3	tres		20	veinte
4	cuatro		30	treinta
5	cinco		40	cuarenta
6	seis		50	cincuenta
7	siete		60	sesenta

8	ocho		70	setenta
9	nueve		80	ochenta
10	diez		90	noventa
11	once		100	cien
12	doce		1000	mil
13	trece		1,000,000	millón

Other numbers are made by adding two numbers

10 + 6	diez y seis or dieciseis
10 + 7	diez y siete or diecisiete
20 + 1	veinte y uno or veintiuno

Ordinal Numbers

first	primero (a)		seventh	séptimo (a)
second	segundo (a)		eighth	octavo (a)
third	tercero (a)		ninth	noveno (a)
fourth	cuarto (a)		tenth	décimo (a)
fifth	quinto (a)		eleventh	undécimo
sixth	sexto (a)		twelfth	duodécimo

A.3 TIME EXPRESSIONS

EXPRESIONES DEL TIEMPO

hour	hora
minute	minuto
second	segundo
at noon	al medio día
at midnight	a la media noche
in the morning[2,3]	por la mañana[2], durante la mañana[3]
in the afternoon	por la tarde, durante la tarde
in the evening	por la noche, durante la noche

The word "time" has three translations

1   What TIME is it?   Qué HORA es?

[2]When "in" is translated as "por," the expression refers to "morning" as a short interval of time, no specific hour.
[3]When "in" is translated as "durante," the expression refers to "morning" as a larger interval of time, but still no specific hour.

In this instance "time" is translated as "hora" (hour).

| 2 | Take the medicine three TIMES a day. | Tome la medicina tres VECES al día. |

Here the word "time" refers to time in a series. It is used for a repeated action. ("Vez) is the singular form of "veces".)

| 3 | I have TIME to see you today. | Tengo TIEMPO para verle hoy. |

"Tiempo" is used to express time in the sense of duration.

| What time is it? | Qué hora es? |

Between the hour and the half hour, *add* the number of minutes to the hour.

Example:

It is 3:00 in the afternoon.[4]	Son las tres de la *tarde*.[4]
It is 3:10. (It is 3 AND 10.)	Son las tres Y diez.
It is 3:30.[5]	Son las tres y *media*.[5]
It is 3:15.[6].	Son las tres y *cuarto*.[6]

Between the half hour and the next hour, *subtract* the number of minutes from the next hour.

Example:

It is 3:40: (it is 4 MINUS 20.)	Son las cuatro MENOS veinte.
It is 3:45.	Son las cuatro menos cuarto.
It is 3:55.	Son las cuatro menos cinco.

The third-person plural form of the verb "ser" (to be) is "son." When telling time, this form is used with every hour except 1 o'clock, for which the singular form "es" is used.

Example:

| It is 1:00. | Es la una. |

[4]When a specific hour is given,

in the morning		de la mañana
in the afternoon	are translated as	de la tarde
in the evening		de la noche

[5]*media*: one-half, 30 minutes.
[6]*cuarto*: one-quarter, 15 minutes.

It is 1:20.	Es la una y veinte.
It is 1:30.	Es la una y media.
It is 12:50.	Es la una menos diez.

A.4 COLORS

What color is it?

red
white
green
blue
black
brown
gray
yellow
purple
pink

COLORES

De qué color es?

rojo (a)
blanco (a)
verde
azul
negro (a)
café
gris
amarillo (a)
morado (a)
rosado (a)

A.5 CONTRASTING ADJECTIVES

large
small

tall (for height)
short (for height)

high
low

long (for length)
short (for length)

fat
thin

heavy (for weight)
light (for weight)

dark (for colors)
light (for colors)

ADJETIVOS QUE CONTRASTAN

grande
pequeño (a)

alto (a)
bajo (a)

alto (a)
bajo (a)

largo (a)
corto (a)

gordo (a)
flaco (a), delgado (a),
seco (a)

pesado (a)
liviano (a), ligero (a)

oscuro (a)
claro (a)

round	redondo (a)
square	cuadrado (a)
rectangular	rectangular
triangular	triangular
oval	ovalado (a)
smooth	liso (a)
rough	áspero (a), rugoso (a)
regular	regular
irregular	irregular
curly	rizado (a), crespo (a)
straight	liso (a)
soft	suave
hard	duro (a)
tepid	tibio (a)
hot	caliente
boiling	hirviendo
wet	mojado
dry	seco (a)
humid	húmedo (a)
open	abierto (a)
closed	cerrado (a)
painful	doloroso (a)
painless	sin dolor
many	muchos (as)
some	algunos (as)
few	pocos (as)
mobile	móvil
immobile	inmóvil
flat	plano (a)
raised	elevado (a)
central	central
peripheral	periférico (a)

loud	fuerte
soft	suave
weak	débil
strong	fuerte
symmetric	simétrico (a)
asymmetric	asimétrico (a)
better	mejor
worse	peor
the best	lo major
the worst	lo peor
alive	vivo (a)
dead	muerto (a)
healthy	sano (a)
sick	enfermo (a)
sweet	dulce
sour	agrio (a)
bitter	amargo (a)

A.6   WEIGHTS AND MEASURES

PESOS Y MEDIDAS

length	longitud
width	ancho
height	altura
volume	volumen
weight	peso
gram	gramo
kilogram	kilogramo
liter	litro
square millimeter	milímetro cuadrado
square centimeter	centímetro cuadrado
cubic centimeter	centímetro cúbico
millimeter	milímetro
centimeter	centímetro
milligram	miligramo
microgram	microgramo

A.7 PHRASES FOR THE FIRST VISIT

Come in please.
My name is _____.
Who is the patient?
What is your name?
It's nice to meet you.
Did you come alone?
Who brought you?
I would like to talk with
you now.
Later I will examine you.

EXPRESIONES PARA LA PRIMERA VISITA

Entre, por favor.
Me llamo _____.
Quién es el paciente?
Cómo se *llama*?
Mucho *gusto* en conocerle.
Vino *solo* (a)
Quién le trajo?
Me gustaría hablar con
usted ahora.
Más tarde le voy a examinar.

INDEX OF COMMONLY REQUESTED TESTS

amniocentesis	amniocentesis
angiogram	angiograma
angioplasty	angioplastía
arthrogram	arthrograma
arthroscopy	artroscopía
audiogram	audiograma
barium enema	enema de bario
blood gas	gasometría
blood test	prueba de sangre
bone marrow biopsy	bíópsia de la médula ósea
bronchoscopy	broncoscopía
CAT scan	tomografía computada
catheterization, cardiac	cateterismo cardíaco
checkup	chequeo
cholangiogram . . .	colangiograma . . .
endoscopic	endoscopico
percutaneous	percutáneo
colonoscopy	colonoscopía
colposcopy	colposcopía
cystoscopy	cistoscopía
dilatation and curettage	dilatación y legrado
drainage	drenaje
electrocardiogram	electrocardiograma

electroencephalogram	electroencefalograma
electromyography	electromiografía
endoscopy	endoscopía
endoscopic retrograde cholangiopancreatography (ERCP)	colangiopancreatografía retrógrada endoscópica
fluoroscopy	fluroscopía
intravenous pyelogram	pielograma intravenoso
laparoscopy	laparoscopía
laryngoscopy	laringoscopía
magnetic resonance imaging scan	imágenes por resonancia magnétia
mammogram	mamografía
manometry	manometría
monitor . . .	monitor . . .
cardiac	cardíaco
fetal	cardíaco fetal
holter	cardíaco ambulatorio
myelogram	mielograma
Pap smear	examen de Papanicolaou
retrograde pyelogram	pielograma retrógrado
sigmoidoscopy (flexible)	sigmoidoscopía (flexible)
slit-lamp	lámpara de hendidura
sonogram	sonograma
spirometry	espirometría
tomography . . .	tomografía . . .
CT	computada
PET	por emisión de positrones
ultrasound	ultrasonido
urinalysis	examen de orina
urography . . .	urografía . . .
excretory	excretoria
retrograde	retrograda
venogram	venograma
x-ray	radiografía

INDEX OF TERMS

Some terms in this index appear without page numbers. They are included, with the Spanish translation, for reference purposes. An index of verbs follows this index.

Medical history of the family (*antecedentes médicos familiares*), 18–20, 23–24
Medicines (*medicinas*), 23, 82
  contraceptives, 94–100
  for diabetics, 86–89
  hormones, 93
  how to use, 83–84
  index of therapeutic groups (*índice de grupos terapeuticos*), 89–93
  instructions about (*instrucciones sobre las medicinas*), 81–89
  insulin, 81, 86–89, 92
  past use of, 82, 118
  prescription instructions, 82
  side effects, 84–85
  storage instructions, 85–86
Memory, loss of (*pérdida de la memoria*), 54, 132
Menopause (*menopausia*), 47–48
Menstrual history (*historia menstrual*), 45–46
Menstrual period (*regla, período*), 45–46, 47, 49, 96–98, 100, 103
Mental retardation (*retraso mental*), 24, 119
Mental status (*estado mental*), 66, 125–128
Mescaline (*mescalina*), 141
Mild (*leve*), 27, 56, 120
Milk (*leche*), 24, 37, 39, 107, 108
Mineral oil (*aceite mineral*), 108
Miscarriage (*aborto espontáneo*), 102
Moderate (*moderado(a)*), 27, 56, 120
Monitor (*monitor*)
  cardiac (*cardíaco*)
  fetal (*cardíaco fetal*)

holter (*cardíaco ambulatorio*)
Months (*meses del año*), 66, 145–146
Mood (*ánimo*), 133
Mouth (*boca*), 32, 61, 62, 67, 83, 84, 85, 109, 141
Movement, limitation of (*limitación de movimiento*), 30
MRI scan (*imagen por resonancia magnética*), 78
Mucus in stools (*heces con moco*), 37, 39
Multiple births (*nacimientos múltiples*), 102
Mumps (*paperas*), 20
Muscle biopsy (*biopsia de los músculos*), 77
Muscle spasm (*calambre múscular*), 51, 105
Muscle weakness (*debilidad muscular*), 51
Muscles (*músculos*), 65, 105
Musculo-skeletal system (*sistema músculo-esquelético*), 51–52
  chief complaint or review of systems, 51–52
  laboratory examinations, 77
  physical examination, 65–66
Mustard (*mostaza*), 108, 109
Myelogram (*mielograma*), 77
Myocardial infarct (*infarto cardíaco*), 24, 119

Name (*nombre*), 12, 66
Nausea (*náusea*), 34, 37, 39, 56, 85, 86, 91, 103, 109, 113
Neck (*cuello*) see Head and neck
Needles (*agujas*), 22
Nephrologist (*especialista en los riñones*), 78

INDEX OF VERBS

ISBN 0-07-134550-7

9 780071 345507

90000